These Sacred Grounds

Celebrating 150 Years of
St. Agnes Cemetery

Three stained glass windows in the Walsh Family Mausoleum cast beautiful reflections of color on the marble lined floor and crypts. The Walsh Family owned and operated Walsh's Department Store located on State Street in Albany. Renowned for its impeccable service, the store carried a line of fine clothing and furs for Albany's elite.

These Sacred Grounds

Celebrating 150 Years of St. Agnes Cemetery

Kelly Grimaldi

Kelly Grimaldi
Dec. 2018

Albany Diocesan
Cemeteries
A Tradition of Faith

48 Cemetery Avenue
Menands, NY 12204
www.CapitalDistrictCemeteries.org

Developed and Produced by Print Matters Productions, Inc.
Design by Lori S. Malkin Design

Printed in China

ISBN 978-0-9796-6858-6

Cover photographs by Jennifer Mele

Photography Credits:
Archive photos: 37, 38, 47, 65, 85, 86
Kevin Franklin: 60
Kelly Grimaldi: 54, 136, 137, 138–139, 144, 154, 146–147
Mick Hales: 2, 6–7, 13, 16–17, 19, 20, 33, 39, 44, 24–25, 55, 56, 61, 66, 67, 77, 80, 83, 84, 97, 103 (bottom), 106, 112, 119, 120, 128, 134–135, 140, 143, 148–149, 153 (middle, bottom)
Linda Heim: 73
Jeanne Keefe: 70, 107, 157
Library of Congress: 68
Luke McGarry: 160
Jennifer Mele: 8, 10, 18, 21, 23, 26, 28, 29, 30–31, 34–35, 40, 41, 45, 46, 48–49, 53, 59, 69, 88–89, 91, 92–93, 96, 101, 102, 103 (top), 104, 105, 108, 109 (bottom), 111, 114–115, 116, 117, 123, 124 (bottom), 125, 126, 127, 130–131, 141, 142, 151, 152, 153 (top), 155, 158, 159
Chuck Miller: 15, 63, 64, 82, 87, 98–99, 121, 129, 133, 145, 150
Lana Ortiz: 72
Kathleen Quinn: 42
Ken Rohling: 74–75
Spindle City Historic Society Archives: 109 (top)
Rick Touchette: 122, 124 (top)
John Walsh: 71

Contents

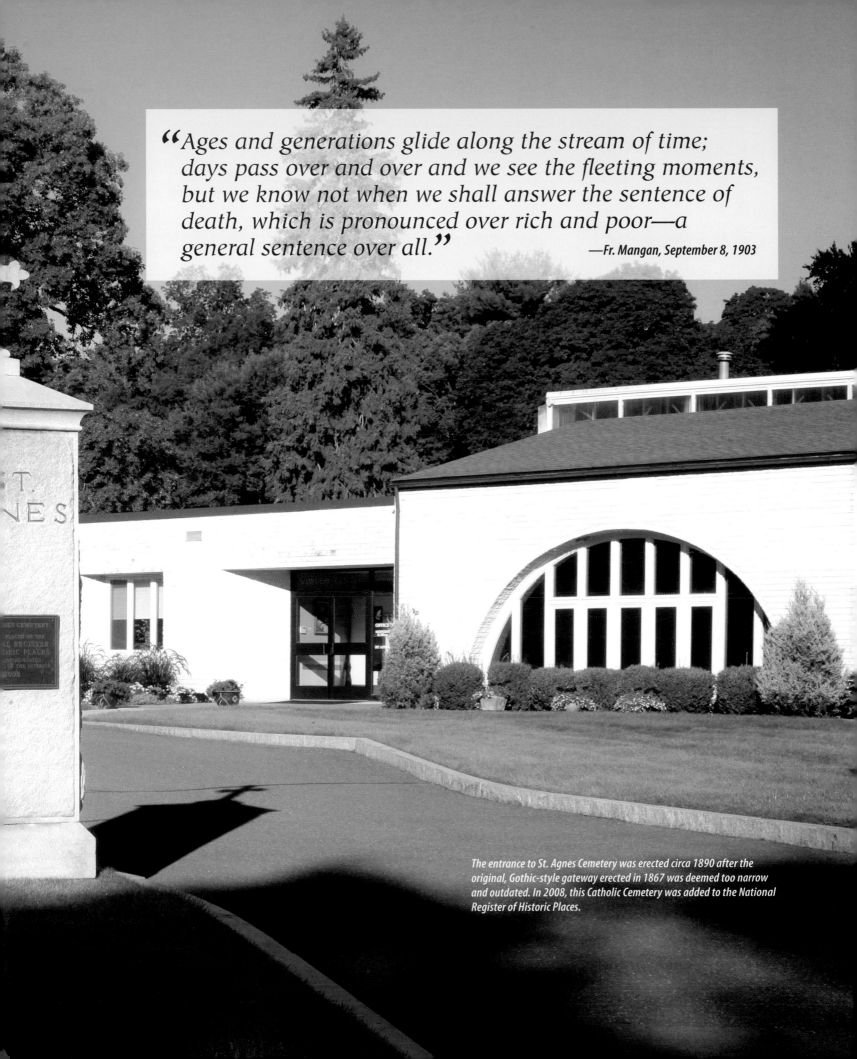

"Ages and generations glide along the stream of time; days pass over and over and we see the fleeting moments, but we know not when we shall answer the sentence of death, which is pronounced over rich and poor—a general sentence over all."

—Fr. Mangan, September 8, 1903

The entrance to St. Agnes Cemetery was erected circa 1890 after the original, Gothic-style gateway erected in 1867 was deemed too narrow and outdated. In 2008, this Catholic Cemetery was added to the National Register of Historic Places.

The Charles F. McGovern Mausoleum was erected in 1929—the year of the stock market crash that marked the start of the Great Depression. Made of large marble blocks and lined with white marble on the interior, this neoclassical style structure features a beautiful stained glass window.

Foreword

INSPIRED BY THE NOVEL VICTORIAN NOTION that cemeteries should be idealized natural landscapes, the founders of St. Agnes Cemetery sought to create for Albany Catholics a beautiful "city of the dead." Emulating the style of English landscape gardens, the architects created "God's Acre," a sublime parkland of winding paths, panoramic vistas, and dappled glades.

Over the next 150 years, St. Agnes became an institution serving both the living and the departed. Tens of thousands of families have buried their beloved dead in her consecrated grounds. As a community of faith, orphans lie in the shadow of the elaborate monuments to titans of industry, and politicians are buried among the faithful with modest headstones.

St. Agnes Cemetery serves as a symbol of the extended community of believers, a community unbroken by death. As a sacred place, St. Agnes serves the faithful and bears witness to all, the hope that we, as Catholic Christians, share in the resurrection. It is a place where the signs and symbols of our Catholic faith are displayed with pride and reverence.

How things have changed since the early days! Almost exclusively Irish in the nineteenth century, decade by decade, all were welcomed. Ornate family estates gave way to smaller lots and the bronze memorials of shrines to memorialize the deceased. Community mausoleums shelter thousands of individual crypts; columbaria and urn gardens reflect the increasing prevalence of cremation.

In many ways, our job remains the same. Our dedicated staff continues the reverent maintenance of the grounds and the compassionate service to the bereaved. Catholic teaching and the preferential option for the poor continue to form our ministry.

When Catholics gather at St. Agnes Cemetery following the death of a loved one, or return to pray and remember, the Church offers consolation, hope, and peace. This tradition of faith will guide us for the next 150 years.

—Rick Touchette, *Executive Director Albany Diocesan Cemeteries*

Preface

AS ITS FIRST HISTORIAN, it is my pleasure to acquaint you with beautiful historic St. Agnes Cemetery located in the Hudson River Valley's village of Menands, New York. This book is written to commemorate the 150th anniversary of the founding of St. Agnes Cemetery in 1867. It is the first book written about the cemetery since Myron A. Cooney edited a book titled *St. Agnes Cemetery: Its Past and Present Associations* published in 1899—one year after he died. To appreciate the significance of the founding of St. Agnes Cemetery, now under the management of Albany Diocesan Cemeteries, it is important for the reader to understand some of the reasons for its establishment. It begins with understanding the concept of the rural cemetery movement in general, as summarized in Chapter 1.

My own Irish immigrant ancestors are resting here. It is a very special place to me, and I remain committed to preserving St. Agnes Cemetery's history for as long as I am able. This book will take you on a walk through the founding of the cemetery to its present day. It was a challenge to write. It spans the time from its establishment two years post-Civil War into modernity and beyond. May it serve as a tribute to the families we have been and are privileged to serve, often times in their darkest hour of grief. It is my hope that this book will be an enduring piece of St. Agnes Cemetery's history. Someday, I, too, will rest in her sacred grounds. I hope that readers will reflect on my words, enjoy the photographs and come to appreciate the serene beauty of this historic place.

—Kelly Grimaldi, *Historian, Albany Diocesan Cemeteries*

This gravestone marks the final resting place of Patrick and Catherine O'Connell.
It was erected in their memory by their great, great granddaughter, Kelly Grimaldi,
historian for St. Agnes Cemetery.

Acknowledgments

I REMEMBER THE FIRST TIME I SAW ST. AGNES CEMETERY after returning to upstate New York from Maine where I had lived for over twenty years. I had forgotten how beautiful it is. I walked the winding roads, visiting my relatives' gravesite and marveling at the collection of monuments, statues, and mausoleums. Fate is a funny thing and here I am working for an organization I deeply respect.

There are so many wonderful people whose help I would like to acknowledge that it would take another book to recognize them all. First, I would like to thank Executive Director Rick Touchette for seeing in me someone worthy of becoming Albany Diocesan Cemeteries' first historian. Each day I am here is a learning experience. Every day I strive to bring the stories of the dead to light to honor their lives and their time in history before they came to eternally rest in peace.

I would like to thank the photographers whose works appear on nearly every page of this book. Mick Hales, a notable professional photographer, helped us early on by sharing his knowledge of the book development process. We are grateful to him for his invaluable advice and referrals and for his photographs featured in this book. Also, thank you to Jennifer Mele, Chuck Miller, the many photography contest participants and a few staff members who brought their talents to these pages and captured the essence of St. Agnes Cemetery through the lenses of their cameras. Their work will now endure for centuries on the pages of this book.

Several people I have been privileged to meet since becoming historian for our cemeteries have contributed narratives to this book. It is a privilege to recognize the good work of the Honorable John (Jack) McEneny, Dr. Kathleen Quinn, Vincent J. Forte, Jr., and Dr. Joseph Meany, all of whom are long-time supporters of St. Agnes Cemetery and have family resting here. Thank you for being part of this book and for your love and commitment to these sacred grounds.

Lastly, I wish to express my deep appreciation for the staff of Albany Diocesan Cemeteries, particularly the St. Agnes operations staff led by Operations Manager Luke McGarry and Assistant Operations Manager Bob Barrows. I'd also like to express my sincere appreciation for our former Assistant Executive Director Tim Putorti, who retired in 2016 after serving the cemeteries for 38 years. I am truly fortunate to call such an ethical, hardworking, and honorable group of people my colleagues.

Many stones removed from St. Mary's Cemetery formerly located on Washington Avenue and from the State Street Burial Grounds (now Washington Park in Albany) were restored to their previous glory. These ornately carved marble stones date back to the 1840s through the 1870s. When cemeteries located in the heart of a progressively urbanized Albany got in the way of development, the bodies and gravestones were moved to St. Agnes Cemetery and other rural cemeteries in the area. Most of the stones are memorials to Irish immigrants with their county of origin and parish inscribed as a matter of national pride. These old stones are historical documents valuable to genealogists.

CHAPTER 1

Founding

CITY DWELLERS LIVED IN THE PRESENCE OF BURIAL GROUNDS for a long time before rural cemeteries were established. Most of Albany's earliest burials were in lots on family farms or in church lots. By the late eighteenth century burials in Albany's church cemeteries were not available because they were full. Random burial places, such as backyard family plots within the heart of an urban center, were no longer appropriate. To address the need for burial space, Albany's Common Council made provisions for municipal cemetery grounds including land that is now Washington Park. These cemeteries accommodated the needs of a rapidly expanding city and solved the problem of what to do with the dead—but only in the short term.

Municipal cemeteries were filling to capacity as early as the 1830s. By the mid-nineteenth century an unprecedented surge of immigrants, many of whom were Catholic, made space in Albany a shrinking commodity. Questions of where to put the dead were of imminent concern. In the 1840s the Albany Cemetery Association's efforts resulted in the creation of Albany Rural Cemetery, the first of its kind in the area, through the acquisition of farmland owned by Thomas Hillhouse and others. It was established as a nondenominational cemetery and not considered appropriate grounds for Catholic burials. There remained a need for a rural Catholic Cemetery. The establishment of St. Agnes Cemetery met that need when it opened in 1868. The nineteenth-century rural cemetery movement launched an effort to establish park-like settings to accommodate an increasing number of bodies requiring burial space. Large tracts of land were engineered with winding pathways and strategically landscaped hillsides and fields that best utilized space while remaining aesthetically appealing. Historic St. Agnes Cemetery located in Albany County, Menands, New York, is an excellent example of the rural cemetery movement's objective.

Saint Anthony holding the Christ child. Carved in marble, the figures have collected a fair share of pollutants and lichen over the past century.

A variety of specimen trees were carefully placed along the winding roads of the original fifty acres. Among them was the Cooper Beech—a behemoth with an impressive reach across the old lots on Founders Hill. Measuring more than five feet in diameter at the base, these gnarly giants lived through more than a century of history. What those coppery leaves have seen! Sadly, they are succumbing to disease as living things are apt to do in old age. Two of them recently came crashing down in wind storms, causing damage to monuments in their paths and to other nearby trees. Seeing something so enormous on the ground looked surreal and sad. We make every effort to proactively address hazardous trees. Sometimes Mother Nature comes in with an overnight sneak attack and our old beauties bear the brunt of her wrath.

Piece by piece, trees planted back in the nineteenth century are leaving sacred ground. Ironically, the same tree service, Davey Tree & Lawn Care Experts, shown here taking down this old maple, likely planted it. Cemetery records show we have had a business relationship with Davey Tree dating way back to the 1880s Tree removal in St. Agnes Cemetery is a yearly event. The view from this worker's "office" must be sublime!

Unlike crowded municipal cemeteries, it provided ample space for the dead that the living enjoyed visiting. This lovely cemetery served a practical function and also reflected changing attitudes toward death and burial that took shape during and after the American Civil War. An obvious change in attitudes toward death and burial is noted in the stylistic differences between funerary iconography and epitaphs featured on gravestones in old church burying grounds and rural cemeteries such as St. Agnes.

Harsh pictorial narratives featuring skeletal remains accompanied by morbid words inscribed on gravestones are not found here. Instead, the visitor is greeted with words of comfort and symbols representing the hope of resurrection etched on commemorative monuments. This is a peaceful, desirable cemetery—a destination rather than something to avoid.

All throughout St. Agnes Cemetery there are burial lots that memorialize the richest and the poorest and everyone in between. These sacred grounds served Catholics of all socioeconomic means, although it is the acres of grandiose monuments and private mausoleums marking the final resting places of upper-class citizens that are of most interest to the modern visitor. Many nineteenth and early twentieth century citizens left permanent, visible evidence of their social status in the community. St. Agnes Cemetery is among the last vestiges of a bygone era bearing testimony to the level of wealth and refinement many Capital District citizens once enjoyed in the early years. Lovely vistas, carefully arranged plantings, and ornately carved memorials detract the visitor from the fact that they are in a silent city for the dead.

Cemeteries tell us things about the social and cultural climate of a given period in history such as wealth disparities and religious conventions dominating communities. Silent stones marking buried remains are not "silent" at all. Funerary art is symbolic and reflects attitudes relating to death and the hope of resurrection, as do gravestone inscriptions. Carved words in stone also provide statistical data important to the study of epidemic disease patterns, average life spans for adults, infant/maternal mortality rates, ethnic patterns of migration, and so on. Grave markers are learning tools and key components in the analysis of the past, making them significant to material culture historians.

 ## Our Founder: Irony and Persistence in the Early Days of St. Agnes Cemetery

In the transcription of deeds related to the land acquisition of the St. Agnes Cemetery's original fifty acres, it is stated that Peter Cagger, a well-respected, successful attorney from Albany, purchased the land on the twenty-eighth day of March in the year of our Lord one thousand eight hundred and sixty seven from Joseph D. Badgley and Eliza H.,

◀ The steps leading up to St. Agnes's founder Peter Cagger's final resting place.

▶ On a foggy morning in 2016, the gravesite for Peter Cagger, founder of St. Agnes Cemetery, stands as solid and sturdy as the day it was erected in 1868.

his wife. The price for this land was twenty thousand dollars. Mr. Cagger promptly resold the land for the sum of one dollar for the purpose of establishing Albany County's first Catholic rural cemetery. Cagger worked tirelessly in collaboration with an esteemed board of trustees to make their vision of a beautifully designed park-like cemetery a reality.

Landscape architects and engineers transformed the rocky, hilly land into one of the most beautiful Catholic cemeteries in the nation in just twelve months. St. Agnes Cemetery was consecrated on May 19, 1868. Cagger was elected the first president of the board of trustees and was given first choice of grave lots. He chose well in June 1868. Cagger's cemetery lot is a large parcel of grass high upon what we now call Founders' Hill. The view from his lot is spectacular.

In an ironic twist of fate, the cemetery's founder and first trustee-president was among its very first interments. Peter Cagger was killed in an accident one month after choosing his final resting place. His grave is marked with a two-story high granite obelisk topped with a Latin cross and massive steps flanked by equally impressive granite urns.

So much was written about Mr. Cagger in the days following his death that it makes no sense to try and rewrite details from a twenty-first-century viewpoint. Victorian-era journalists, with their flair for the dramatic and sentimental, flowery words, give us clear insight into the character of the man and the circumstances surrounding his death. An excerpt from an article titled "Melancholy Accident"

published in the *New York Herald* (New York, New York) on Wednesday, July 8, 1868 (Volume: XXXIII, Issue 190) is a good example, and provided here:

On Monday night last, about half-past twelve o'clock, Peter Cagger, of Albany, the distinguished lawyer and democratic politician, was accidently killed while driving in Central Park. Shortly after having entered the Park they reached [he was riding with his friend John Develin] a sharp curve in the road, and as they drove briskly around it the spokes of one of the wheels gave away upsetting the vehicle and throwing its occupants to the ground. Mr. Cagger was thrown heavily to the ground striking his head on the roadway. Mr. Cagger's skull was fractured, in fact crushed in and his face slightly cut.

Peter Cagger adopted the profession of law, rose rapidly to a position of great eminence and accumulated a large fortune having achieved the reputation of being one of the ablest special pleaders in the State. In addition to this marked talent he is intimately identified with the Democratic Party and for 20 years had been a recognized leader in the organization. But in addition to his marked talent as an accomplished political leader, he possessed the confidence of all classes of men in a degree rarely equaled by men prominent in political life and service. His integrity was beyond question and his honesty, foresight, prudence and zeal insured to him success in his public labors. Mr. Cagger's warm benevolence and geniality of his disposition endeared him in an unusual degree to all who enjoyed his friendship. He leaves a wife and a young family of whom this calamity will fall most heavily. In every walk of life, the deceased was a most estimable man, and the news of his sudden death will cast a gloom over the community where he resided and will be received with deep regret throughout the country.

Each news article repeats the same high praise and regret for the life of a good man cut tragically short. His vision of establishing a magnificent Catholic cemetery was not darkened by his passing. The trustees who worked closely with him mourned

The Cagger lot bathed in the light and color of a glorious fall morning.

THESE SACRED GROUNDS

The Cassidy Family grave lot on Founders'
Hill. William Cassidy took over as the second
president of the board of trustees after his
brother-in-law's sudden demise.

The Enduring Beauty of Zinc Monuments

At first glance, the Clairmont monument looks like it was carved in granite with bronze plates secured to the sides. It is actually hollow and made of pure zinc. Often called "white bronze," this type of memorial first appeared in cemeteries in the mid-1870s, peaking in popularity in the 1880s. Production of zinc monuments ended in 1914 at the start of World War I. The war effort required zinc to produce munitions and thus the production of cemetery monuments ended.

In the 40 or so years that zinc monuments were in production, they never became very popular. In St. Agnes Cemetery, there are only six of them. All of them are in superb condition, like the one featured here. They never rust nor do they attract lichen, mold, or even pollutants, yet people of the era of production could not be convinced they would last. Victorians considered them to be distasteful and cheap looking. Stone carvers of that time did their best to perpetuate the idea that zinc monuments would never endure the elements and withstand the test of time. But these old beauties look better a century later than many of their stone counterparts—especially marble and sandstone.

The Clairmont monument is one of only six zinc monuments in St. Agnes Cemetery.

his loss, but carried on in his name. Cagger's brother-in-law took the reins as the second president, and the growth of St. Agnes Cemetery did not falter. On the contrary, what happened in the next ten years on this sacred ground was astounding. Nearly every lot on the original fifty acres was mapped out and purchased. More land was acquired and developed in the same elegant style that made the cemetery a timeless beauty. Historic St. Agnes Cemetery is among the many enduring legacies of a good and generous Catholic man.

Peter Cagger is gone, but he will never be forgotten.

Building on the Legacy:
Moving Forward with William Cassidy

After Cagger's untimely death, William Cassidy, an astute man highly regarded in the realm of state and national governmental affairs, had a dual role. His first, we must assume, was as a brother helping his grieving sister, Elizabeth (Cassidy) Cagger, come to terms with her recent widowhood. She had young children to raise and although Peter left her very well situated financially, she was still a woman alone in the patriarchal society of the mid-nineteenth century. William no doubt took over the management of his sister's household and finances until she regained her strength. When strong enough to carry on with her life, young Mrs. Cagger partnered with Mary Cagger, Peter's daughter from his first marriage, to found a much-needed hospital in memory of her beloved husband. Hence, we now have St. Peter's Health Partners—one of the largest health organizations in the state. Shortly after founding the hospital, Mrs. Cagger moved with her children to France, where they remained. Descendants of Peter and Elizabeth Cagger still reside in Europe as of this writing.

Cassidy's second responsibility to the Cagger legacy was to ensure it moved forward in the form of a successfully established and well-maintained Catholic cemetery. He was nominated the second president of the board of trustees and having chosen—without any apparent superstitious trepidation—his own final resting place next to the Cagger lot, Cassidy erected one of the most magnificent memorials to grace Founders' Hill. He led a full and industrious life as the respected part owner and sole editor of the *Albany Atlas* (which later merged with *The Albany Argus*), a Democratic daily newspaper. He served as editor in chief for thirty years and his tenure as president of St. Agnes Cemetery's board of trustees ended only with his death on January 23, 1873.

William Cassidy is gone, but he will never be forgotten.

Early Finances

The original book of minutes of the board of trustees is well preserved and safely stored in a fireproof vault. Its yellowed pages are filled with flowery penmanship in faded fountain ink, giving us extraordinary accounts of what would have been considered in its time just ordinary, everyday business. It is the finest account of cemetery history from its opening entry in 1868 until 1895.

Under a category titled "The Finances," it is noted that the total number of interments since the cemetery's organization up to the close of 1885 was 13,096. Using the same time frame for the following account reports, we find a total of $213,573.90 came from lot sales, making St. Agnes Cemetery a very fiscally sound organization in its early years. It was also a generous charitable organization, having advanced $12,000 from its treasury to benefit St. Peter's Hospital and $7,743 to St. Vincent's Male Orphan Asylum. The minutes plainly note it was the intention of the founders to use any surplus monies for charitable work. St. Agnes continues to this day to support other institutions within and outside the Catholic Diocese.

A report in the minutes under the category of "Grounds" notes that in 1885 grave space was sold for 39 cents per square foot. (Currently, the price per square foot is approximately $34, depending on the location of the grave lot.) The cost of grounds maintenance was $20,000 and the cemetery spent $12,212.51 on cemetery improvements. An inventory list of property belonging to St. Agnes Cemetery is particularly quaint as it speaks to the simplicity of doing business in the Victorian era. It is

The executive committee report dated March 10, 1886 consists of a brief overview of the work of St. Agnes Cemetery since its founding. The cemetery received its charter from the New York State Legislature on May 9, 1867.

a long list of everything, from one horse named Agnes, to a plough that does not work, landscape tools, and, of course, a collection of shovels for grave digging. An inventory list today would not include a horse or a broken plough, but we do still have quite a collection of shovels.

Above, left: *Part of the finance report given to the board on March 10, 1886. The interment report also includes the number of interments from 1868 to 1882, showing an average of 230 burials a year. The report continues on page 467 and includes the years 1883–85 and January–February 1886 for a total of 4,627 burials since the first burials on June 2, 1868, making it a very active nineteenth-century cemetery for the area.*

Above, right: *The board of trustee minutes dated June 3, 1885 note that more land for burials would be needed. The William Hart farm (also known as Fernwood) is mentioned as a possible purchase. The land totaled 75 acres including a mansion, stables, and a pond and was eventually purchased in March 1900 for $60,000. A Victorian-style mansion with an interior finished in hardwoods, including rosewood, mahogany, cherry, and maple, was converted into a chapel by Bishop Burke. The cost of the mansion's upkeep was too great a financial burden on the cemetery, and the decision was made to tear it down and convert the land to burial space. Fernwood Pond was left intact. In 1903, it would become the scene of a tragedy. This sad event is discussed in Chapter 3.*

The eclectic styles of monuments in St. Agnes Cemetery make for an interesting walk through time. Enormous granite crosses juxtaposed with respectable marble monoliths, majestic angels, and quaint little lambs each command attention in their own right. The visitor is never bored with the view.

CHAPTER 2

Irish, Catholic, Politics, and Beer

The Nevilles: Prospering in Ireland and America

It is a misconception to assume all people fleeing Ireland in the 1800s arrived on American soil as poor wretches wrought with hunger, sickly and helpless. Many families were very well off and continued to lead successful, prosperous lives in their adopted country.

Such was the case with the Neville Family, as evidenced by the stately monument erected in their memory. The sculpture's contrapposto stance and flowing drapery are reminiscent of an ancient Roman sculpture, indicating the family who commissioned it had substantial wealth and refined taste.

Among the Neville's ancestors are Sir Geoffrey Neville of Waterford, whose name is found on the Charter of Waterford dated 1205 A.D. Nearly five centuries later, we find Thomas J. Neville, a staunch Democrat active in the volatile political scene of the 1870s, accepting the position of clerk of the Board of Public Works. Mr. Neville's character is described as scrupulously faithful to every trust and unwearied persistence in the discharge of his duty. He had many friends in Albany and led the life of a happy bachelor until his heart gave out on June 3, 1886 at the relatively young age of 43 years old. All that is left of his memory is a remarkable female figure standing high upon her stone pedestal and gazing northward to the heavens that are no longer visible through the century-old trees.

The Neville Family's stately monument.

Michael N. Nolan, Albany's first Irish Catholic mayor, died from heat exhaustion on May 31, 1905. He was 72 years old.

Quinn and Nolan

By John J. McEneny

In the uncertain economy of the nineteenth century, the ability to provide regular employment and steady income to workers and their families translated into social prestige, and if skillfully managed, could often lead to political power as well. Such was the case of the several successful brewers whose remains rest in St. Agnes Cemetery, but none more so than the Quinns and Nolans.

The story starts with James Quinn, whose inscription on his Gothic-style obelisk proudly recalls his roots in Edgeworthstown, County Longford, Ireland. Quinn came to Albany in the early 1830s and founded his brewery in 1845 in North Albany, near the Erie Canal's "Little Basin." He would later be joined in the business by his son, Terence John, who was born and educated in Albany and who was active as a volunteer in the local militia and volunteer fire companies.

In the decade prior to the Civil War, American society was divided on many fronts, not the least of which was fear and resentment of immigrants. The face of Albany was becoming more and more diverse in language, religion, and ethnicity, especially during and after the Great Famine in Ireland (1845–1852). Two million sick and desperate Irish people had been driven by hunger and poverty to flee Ireland. Most came to North America, nearly overwhelming the resources of cities like Albany and Troy. Nativist members of the "Know Nothing" Party actively campaigned against the newcomers, often denying them housing, employment, and political influence.

It fell to the earlier immigrants, like the Quinns, who had finally prospered in the days following the development of the Erie Canal and railroads, to provide jobs, and through their support of the charities and good works of the Catholic Church, desperately needed social services. For the impoverished laborer, especially one with a family, a steady job in the labor-intensive brewing industry was not just an opportunity, it could mean survival. Similarly, financial backing from a local brewer could enable entrepreneur saloonkeepers to rise to the middle class.

Terence Quinn's brother-in-law was another Irishman, Michael Nicholas Nolan, whose family had come to the city from Bagenalstown in County Carlow. As a young man, he had joined the California Gold Rush and worked as a manager of a street railway company in San Francisco. On returning to Albany, Nolan gave up his original goal of being a lawyer, married Ann Elizabeth Quinn, and entered her family business, becoming a brewer. After James Quinn's passing the name of the growing company was changed to Quinn and Nolan. The brewery prospered, and a second facility, Beverwyck Brewery, was built next door to produce lager. (Quinn and Nolan only produced ale and porter. Schaefer Brewery would buy out the entire complex in the early 1950s.)

Both men had colorful personalities and were fast friends, intensely loyal to each other. Also, both men were politically ambitious. In an age when men of their lineage were not expected to serve in politics beyond the ward level, Michael Nolan served as fire commissioner in Albany from 1869 to 1878, and his father had served as Albany's overseer of the poor.

The Beverwyck Brewery was built next door to the original brewery to produce lager. Quinn and Nolan had only produced ale and porter.

Terence Quinn's military career as a Lieutenant in the elite Albany Burgesses Corps and Albany 25th Regiment was well known and greatly respected (he is believed to have been the first Union soldier to capture a Confederate prisoner). But his subsequent service, capture, and brief imprisonment while a lieutenant colonel of Irish Civil War soldiers in the unsuccessful 1866 Fenian invasion of Canada raised his profile to a whole different level.

Thanks to anti-British sentiments among the growing constituency of immigrant and first-generation Irish voters, Quinn's political success was all but assured. A staunch Democrat, he served in Albany's Common Council from 1869 to 1872 and in the State Assembly in 1873. In 1876, Terence John Quinn, still senior partner in a growing and successful brewery, was elected to be the first of several Irish Catholics to represent Albany in the US Congress.

Tragically, Terence Quinn never lived to even finish his two-year term in the House of Representatives. His health had reportedly been failing since his Civil War service, during which it was thought he had contracted malaria. In 1878, at the height of his political and professional career, he returned to his hometown and died at the age of 41. His funeral and its procession attracted literally thousands of mourners accompanied by scores of civic and military memorials. He was laid to rest with military honors in the Quinn family plot overlooking the rolling hills of St. Agnes Cemetery.

Terrence J. Quinn (1836–1878) was elected to Congress in 1876 at age 40. He was Representative of New York's 16th District.

Michael Nolan, heartbroken at the loss of his friend, business partner, and political ally, made every effort to blend the Quinn and Nolan families into one. A father of seven children in his own right, he addressed the plight of his widowed sister-in-law and her three children. He managed the family business and acted as guardian whenever needed. He saw to the education of the three Quinn children, who went to elite Catholic boarding schools and colleges with their Nolan cousins.

In 1878, Michael Nolan broke yet another perceived barrier to Irish Catholic and became the first Catholic mayor of Albany. His three terms of office were marked by extensive and lasting public works, especially those benefitting the poor and working class of the city. He completed four new public schools, and in a project we can scarcely appreciate today, he had a viaduct constructed to carry more than one hundred trains daily above Broadway in the congested neighborhood north of the city's downtown. The elimination of that dangerous grade crossing did more than improve traffic; it saved lives, especially the lives of children.

Nolan also made history by being elected in 1880 to serve in Congress. He held the position for two years while still serving as mayor of Albany! He did not run for reelection. He continued as mayor until 1883, when he was forced to resign by a court order. The decision reversed the result of his third election by throwing

THESE SACRED GROUNDS

The Terence John Quinn lot is a large 24-grave family lot in section 21. This stone suffered the ravages of time and was nearly solid black in color and its inscription illegible. An extensive restoration project initiated by the great grandchildren of Terence Quinn commenced in the summer of 2014. Today it is as impressive a memorial as it was when erected more than 130 years ago.

▲ *Close-up view of some of the elaborate iconography on the Terence John Quinn family lot. This 18-foot Gothic-style marble stone was completely restored in 2014.*

▶ *Stained glass window in the Michael Nolan mausoleum.*

out votes deemed to be fraudulent. The election was belatedly awarded to his Republican opponent, Dr. John Swinburne, who served the last seven months of the term.

In 1880, Albany's City Hall, which doubled as the County Court House, caught on fire, and burned beyond saving. The magnificent building, which stands today, was designed by H. H. Richardson, and is no doubt the most visible and beloved reminder of the Nolan administration.

Michael Nolan's final years were spent managing his successful brewery and banking interests at National Savings Bank, while dividing his time between his townhouse on the Ten Broeck Triangle at the foot of Arbor Hill and in his magnificent mansion on Circular Street in Saratoga Springs, where he was an integral part of the racing society. He was famous for his prized thoroughbred, Bourke Cochran.

Nolan died in 1905 at age 72 and is entombed with several family members in his classically designed mausoleum in St. Agnes, appropriately located next door to Martin Glynn, another child of famine era-immigrants, and New York's first Catholic Governor.

The Quinn Family Reflects on Rediscovering Roots

By Kathleen Quinn

In 2013, nine members of the Quinn family met in Albany for the first time. Though we knew our family originated in Albany, we had very little knowledge of our history in Albany, or our family story there. As our dear friend, Jack McEneny, has said, "our history was hidden from us."

We first visited St. Agnes Historic Cemetery to pay our respects to our elders in the Quinn plot and in the Nolan Mausoleum. We were enchanted with the cemetery and immediately felt a bond with our elders. My brother, Michael Quinn, is an amazing double for Terence John Quinn (TJ), our great-grandfather. When Mike first found TJ's name on the obelisk, he touched it, and I was fortunate to have photographed that moment.

Our enchantment quickly dimmed by the state of things in our plot and mausoleum: headstones were tipping over and their inscriptions illegible, the stone obelisk had sugared and was in desperate need of repair, and Jesus, on top of the obelisk, was missing his legs. In the mausoleum, water stood on the floor. The lovely Victorian glass was starting to buckle and a few panes were broken.

St. Agnes historian Kelly Grimaldi was immensely helpful in finding the bank trust that was supposed to have been caring for our plot and mausoleum. We soon embarked on a major restoration of the plot. Three stones had to be completely replaced. The interesting and challenging task was learning what had been written upon them. Friends from afar went to great lengths to help us in our research.

The Quinn Family visited St. Agnes Historic Cemetery to pay their respects to their elders in the Quinn plot and in the Nolan Mausoleum. Great-grandson Michael Quinn touches the inscription on the large Gothic-style marble monument as it was before the extensive restoration process began on the lot.

Throughout our restoration, we all learned a tremendous amount about cemeteries, granite, marble, acid rain, Victorian stained glass, etching in stone, and much more. We truly enjoyed our relationship with the artisans who performed the restorations, and will most likely remain in touch with them for years to come. The cemetery staff were exceptionally helpful throughout what became a very emotional and complex process.

The research required to label the stones correctly grew exponentially, and as the research continued, our elders came to life. Through our investigations, we have learned much about the story of the Quinn and Nolan families and their history in New York. Rather than just names carved in stone, those elders emerged as people. They are now part of our family thread, and it has been an honor to restore their resting place into dignity once again.

As was a tradition in the 1800s, we Quinn cousins celebrated the restoration by returning to Albany the following fall and enjoyed a Victorian picnic at the family plot. Many of the artisans who completed the lovely restoration work and many new Albany friends joined us in the festivities. Most important of all, for those of us who first visited Albany, and who have returned so many times, we have become a much closer family. Our treasured friend, Norman Rice, predicted that following our first visit, we would all remain in touch, though some of us had not met before, and some hadn't seen one another since childhood. Norman was right. No longer are we just a group of cousins that met in Albany on a whim; we are a loving family, connected by our elders in a profound way.

Now that most of our restoration is complete, the Quinn family has had a number of celebrations at our plot, admiring the improvements and always enjoying the beauty of St. Agnes. During the restoration, two dedicated volunteers, Don and Abbie, kindly cleaned a World War I stone in our plot. To repay the favor, we continue on, cleaning whatever needs to be cleaned. On my last visit, I spotted a lovely little angel on the side of a hill. Like so much of our plot before restoration, she is dark with the mildew of age. Soon she will be a shining white marble beacon on the hill, within sight of our plot, for our family.

Albany is now a place where our family gathers, where we have made wonderful friends, learned of its history, and where we feel so completely at home.

The Quinn family is back. To stay.

▲ Daniel O'Connell, veteran of World War I and the son of a Republican saloon owner, become known in Albany as the political boss of the Democratic Machine. His power over Albany lasted for more than four decades. O'Connell, who died in 1977, and his wife, Leta Burnside, who died in 1963, rest in this lot marked with a Tennessee marble monument. The urns flanking his gravestone are occasionally filled with flowers from people in the community who remember "Uncle Dan" fondly.

▶ The Hoellinger Celtic Cross is the largest and most ornately decorated free-standing monument in the cemetery. Erected after the death of his beloved wife Catharine Arts, who died October 14, 1890 at age 62, John Hoellinger had a beautiful tribute to her memory carved into the back of this stone. John died twelve years later at age 80. No children were born of this marriage and the couple had very few living relatives. John died in his home alone with only his maid of 21 years by his side. The bulk of his estate was to be divided among his servants.

THESE SACRED GROUNDS

 ### New York's First Irish Catholic Governor

Like Mayor Michael Nolan, Governor Martin Glynn put fair wages and safe working conditions at the top of his political agenda. He himself came from rural Valatie, New York, where his Irish immigrant parents owned a saloon. He knew firsthand the plight of working men and women in the late nineteenth and early twentieth centuries.

Within fifteen months of taking the office of governor, Glynn successfully established the State Employment Agency, workers' compensation benefits, Department of Food and Marketing to help farmers profit from their labor, and made enormous strides in the improvement of transportation systems (highways and canals) statewide. He cut the fat in state government programs and proved himself to be well adept at managing state finances. His deep budget cuts made for a more progressive and fiscally sound New York State during his brief administration.

Martin Glynn, New York's first Irish Catholic governor, rests in a private mausoleum located next to Michael Nolan, Albany's first Irish Catholic mayor. Glynn's wife, Mary, and their only child, the infant Ruth, rest with him along with members of Mary's family. Governor Glynn was an ethical man of good judgment and compassion. Tragically, he died by his own hand after having suffered for most of his life from pain caused by an injury to his lower spine before he entered college. The pain was often so severe Glynn was rendered an invalid for weeks at a time. On December 14, 1924, Martin Glynn had enough. His death certificate notes his death was caused by suicide by firearm. His bereaved wife, devoted servants and the attending physician knew of the cause, but out of deep love and respect for him, Glynn's cause of death was kept a secret for a long time.

John Heenan: First American Heavyweight Champion

John Heenan's strength was first noticed by an English trainer named Jim Cusick, who introduced him to the sport of prizefighting. The prize ring was outlawed in America and in England in the 1850s, but on April 17, 1860, at Farnborough in Hampshire, a match with the six-foot two-inch, 200-pound Heenan and his challenger, British champion Tom Sayers, an older, shorter, and lighter opponent, went forty-two rounds over a two-hour period.

◀ *Martin Glynn, New York's first Irish Catholic governor rests in a private mausoleum located next to Michael Nolan, Albany's first Irish, Catholic mayor. Glynn's wife Mary and their only child, the infant Ruth, rest with him, joined by members of Mary's family.*

▶ *John Heenan was the first American to win a heavyweight champion belt.*

It was a bloodbath that finally had to conclude when police intervened to prevent Heenan from strangling Sayers to death against the ropes. The referee called the fight a draw. Heenan was outraged and accused Sayers of colluding with the police as soon as it was apparent that the champ from Britain could not win. A rematch was not possible due to irreparable damage done to Sayers's arm. Each fighter was awarded a championship belt, making Heenan the first American to win a heavyweight champion belt.

His career in prizefighting was short-lived. In 1865, he returned to America for good and married actress Sarah Stevens. By 1873, Heenan was ill with tuberculosis and left New York for the cleaner air of Wyoming. He died there on October 28, 1873, with his old manager Jim Cusick by his side. It was Cusick who brought Heenan's body back to New York for burial in St. Agnes Cemetery.

The monument marking John Heenan's final resting place.

CHAPTER 3

Accidental Deaths in Industrialized Albany

UNREGULATED WORKING CONDITIONS IN FACTORIES and other industries utilizing human resources allowed tragedy to strike with regularity. Aside from everyday occurrences of injury—minor and debilitating—there was a shockingly high rate of workplace deaths. Rail workers were crushed by cars; canal workers drowned; factory laborers were sucked into machinery and mangled to death; fires swept through factories, hotels, and breweries, and trapped employees burned.

The City of Albany saw more than its fair share of sad events that ended in the loss of innocent workers. Among the saddest happenings in Albany's history were the December 30, 1894 Delavan House [Hotel] fire and the collapse of Myers Department Store on August 8, 1905. Both disasters were the result of human error and poor building construction. Between these two national news-making events, 29 workers lost their lives.

Splendid Accommodations and Decadent Dining: The Delavan House in Albany

For more than 44 years the Delavan House was the place to be and be seen. On the evening of December 30, 1894, the hotel was especially lively. Politicians and their wives, newspaper people, industry captains, and wealthy land barons had gathered for an event for the candidacy of several men for speaker of the assembly. It was a scene that had often occurred in the famous hotel's history. Ladies and gentlemen of the upper echelons of society mingled among their peers in the grand lobby, elegant tap room, and opulent dining room. Guests wanted for nothing. Servant girls and young porters discretely stood in the wings waiting to be summoned or dismissed with a careless wave of a hand. Delavan House glittered at the height of the Victorian era—a time when unprecedented wealth and unimaginable poverty were accepted as the natural order of things. Neither guest nor servant had any warning their lives were about to be changed forever. At approximately 8:30 p.m. on that cold winter's night, the opulent hotel began its rapid devastation that continues to fascinate historians today. Delavan House burned to the ground.

The next day every major newspaper throughout the country featured headlines and detailed accounts of the fire. With the usual Victorian flair for drama, the demise of Albany's famous hotel was retold until fiction clouded a truth that needed no embellishment. Seconds after the first whiff of smoke was detected, cries of fire could be heard in all parts of the hotel. A state of panic gripped guests and sent them into a wild frenzy as they searched frantically for a means to escape. According to one newspaper account people on the upper floors could not avail themselves of the exits, for the flames were rushing along the corridors and forcing them to hang out of windows or dangle on insufficient rope fire escapes. Horse-drawn fire carts arrived within ten minutes, but ladders were not high enough to reach the upper two floors. It took only fifteen minutes for the entire structure to be wrapped in flames. Most of the guests were rescued or were able to escape unharmed.

Only one fatality made the newspapers although a total of sixteen people lost their lives that fateful night. Newspaper articles reported that Mrs. Henry F. Fooks (also spelled Foakes), wife of the agent of the American Cash Register company of Dayton, Ohio "was the only death, she dying at the hospital after having jumped from a fourth story window while her husband clung to the rope fire escape." Aside from the tragic death of Mrs. Fooks, reporters wrote sympathetically about the terror hotel guests experienced while escaping the flames. Some newspaper articles made brief or nonchalant remarks about the loss of hotel staff. Compassionate words used to describe Mrs. Fooks's demise were never used in connection with the other fifteen people who died. Invisible as they were in life, they were even more so in death.

It is documented that the hotel's proprietors could not ascertain who was on the payroll that evening. Payroll records burned with the hotel and since many employees were poor immigrants with no family living nearby—nobody was looking for them. The dead were initially described only by their occupations: servants, chambermaids, a pantry girl, two "colored" cooks, and a steward.

Many of the fifteen dead remained unaccounted for until the last bit of ruins were cleaned off the site in April 1895. It was then, over four months later, the charred bodies of Irish immigrants Norah Sullivan, 28, and her sister Mary, 21, were found near each other. They were trapped on the fifth floor along with fellow chambermaids Bridget Fitzgibbons and Kate Crowley. The hotel's proprietors were forced to conclude that several of their employees had perished in the fire. No lawsuits were filed, no insurance compensation was paid out, and little attention beyond the initial news media sensationalism was paid to the demise of the hotel workers.

 ### Five Floors of Fashion and Finery: Myers Department Store

Nearly eleven years after Albany's grandest hotel burned, Myers Department Store on North Pearl Street collapsed and was reduced to a pile of iron, timber, and brick. Hindsight tells us the collapse was inevitable given the five-story building's unstable structure and owing to the astounding incompetence of the people overseeing its renovation. A newspaper article found in the *Watertown Daily Times* printed the day after the Myers Department Store tragedy quotes contractor John Dyer, Jr.:

> *I had the contract for the work that was being done at the Myers store. We were enlarging the basement and building lockers and a cloak room for the use of employees of the store. There was excavation done but none that I know of that would weaken the walls. I could not say offhand what the thickness of the walls were. None of our work gave way and I cannot account for the accident, which is most unfortunate indeed. I did not consider the work extraordinarily hazardous but took great precaution against an accident as will be shown.*

Contractor John Dyer, Jr. was defending himself to the press as he would have to do for months following the tragedy. He stated to the press, "I feel sure it will be shown later that it was through no fault of mine that the accident occurred. I

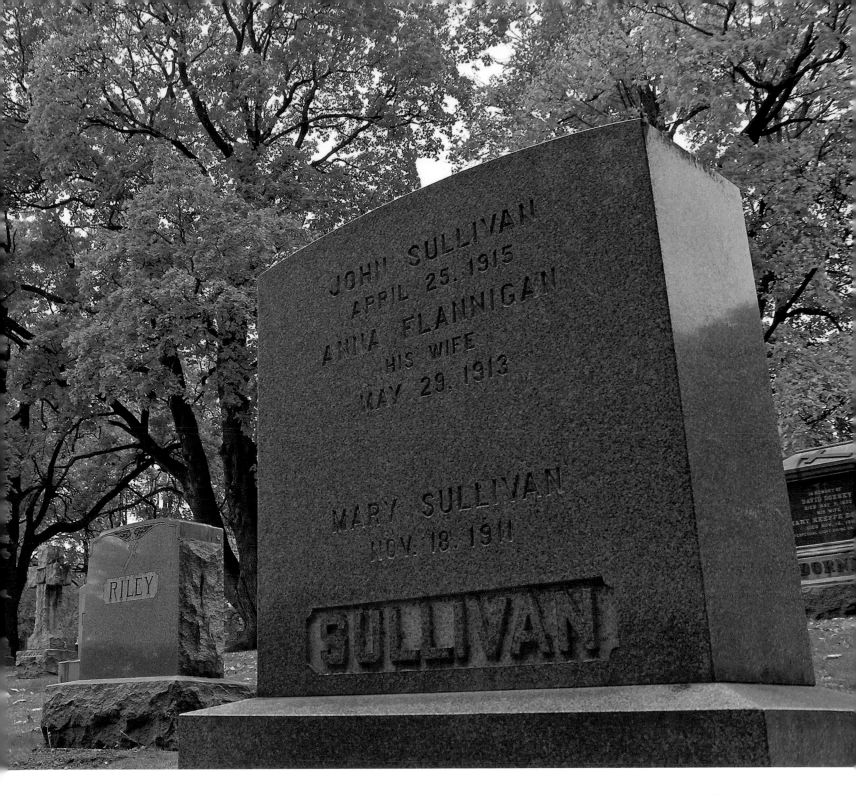

JOHN SULLIVAN
APRIL 25, 1915
ANNA FLANNIGAN
HIS WIFE
MAY 29, 1913

MARY SULLIVAN
NOV. 18, 1911

SULLIVAN

RILEY

do not believe the loss of life will be anything like what has been reported." Renowned architect Marcus Reynolds, the designer of several of Albany's largest buildings, made a statement in the same newspaper article that counters the contractor's statement. It is paraphrased in summary here:

The charred remains of Norah Sullivan, 28, and her sister, Mary, 21, were interred together unceremoniously in April 1895 in St. Agnes Cemetery. Their names were never inscribed on the family monument. (The Mary Sullivan noted on the monument is most likely the mother of the young women who died in the fire).

The calamity at Myers Department Store is just what might have been expected. North Pearl Street is lined with old ramshackle buildings that have been remodeled, altered and their walls made to bear weights they were never intended to support. The original walls were built in former days when hardly anyone knew what good work was. The mortar was poor . . . walls were weakened with repeated alterations much like as was done in the case of John Myers company. The operation was extremely precarious and attended with danger.

Thirteen people died the day the walls came raining down. One large iron beam took the lives of four girls. In an instant, all the promises of youth were snuffed out. The youngest victim was a boy named Francis Leonard. He was only twelve years old when Myers Department store crushed his thorax. It was of no consolation to the victims'

families that the most competent man in the state, C. L. Daggett, was supervising the work on the department store. His competence quickly came under question. Neither John Dyer nor Daggett claimed the event was anything more than an unforeseen and unfortunate accident. The citizens of Albany and the legal system begged to differ.

The store's collapse was investigated and it was determined by structural engineers and architects, experts appointed by Albany's Mayor Gaus, that the contractor placed defective supports under the central portion of the building during the course of repairs. Headlines generated by the Associated Press in November 1905 read: BOTH WERE INDICTED. The Albany County grand jury indicted John Dyer, Jr., the contractor, and Clark L. Daggett, his supervising architect, charging them with manslaughter in the second degree. They faced fifteen years in prison if convicted. Both men remained out on bail pending trial. Regardless

THESE SACRED GROUNDS

of the outcome of any criminal trial, Dyer and Daggett had to know in their hearts that their questionable judgment caused thirteen young people to perish on a summer's day.

The only positive development to come out of the building's collapse was the establishment of a bureau of code enforcement. Building collapses were not uncommon and too many people died in preventable disasters.

The store's founder, John G. Myers, died in 1901. In his worst nightmare, he could not have imagined the horrific scene that played out in Albany on August 8, 1905. His body rests in Albany Rural Cemetery in a grave marked by a magnificent eight-foot-tall bronze angel. In St. Agnes Cemetery, located on the other side of the fence from Albany Rural Cemetery, eight out of thirteen victims of the collapsed store rest in peace.

Twelve-year-old Francis Leonard, fifteen-year-old John E. Powers, nineteen-year-old Mary McEvoy, twenty-year-old Katharine M. Cashman and Minnie C. Bulman, twenty-one-year-old Helen J. Malone, twenty-three-year-old Alice L. Sharpe, and forty-six-year-old Michael J. Fitzgerald are gone but not forgotten.

◀ *Alice L. Sharpe, age 23, was crushed in the Myers Department Store Building collapse on August 5, 1905. She is one of eight victims buried in St. Agnes Cemetery. Families received $1,500 in insurance money for each of the victims. It was considered blood money by most and used to erect impressive monuments for the unfortunate victims.*

▶ *At age 12, Francis Leonard was the youngest victim of the Myers collapse. He worked as a cash boy for the store.*

Gone too Soon: Sammy Severino's Story

Samuel Severino's name should not be on page 45 of an interment book for St. Agnes Cemetery. Based on the average lifespan of an American male, he should have died sometime in the 1990s. He could have even made it into the millennium. One split-second decision, a dumb one like we all make from time to time, cost him his life.

Sammy's life was typical for the son of Italian immigrant farmers. His parents had six other boys in addition to Sammy, and three girls. I would not have paid any attention to Sammy if not for Nicolina (Lena) Santalucia Campagna, who is nearing 100 years old at the time of this writing. In 2014, she, through emails from her daughter, Patti Kopach, contacted me to locate the gravesite of her cousin, whom she remembers fondly. She wished to visit his grave and pay her respects. I pulled the interment card for Samuel Severino, and from that moment Patti Kopach and I began an extensive email conversation. His interment card says Sammy's death was a result of an automobile accident. Accidents are a common cause of death, according to our cemetery records. But visits from someone who remembers attending the funeral of a child who died nearly eight decades ago is not a common occurrence. Lena knew the story of this kid Sammy, and I wanted to hear it. About a year later, I met Sammy's nephew, sixty-five-year-old Jimmy Severino, and we put a few more pieces of Sammy's life together.

Lena recalls Sammy lived with his parents (her aunt and uncle) and nine siblings on a pig farm off Western Avenue. His address was listed as Stop 5 Western Avenue, but the home, one of the first duplexes in Albany, was actually located off of Russell Road. Patti remembers visiting her great uncle as a child and says she remembers the house being neat and tidy, and it did not smell of pigs. Sammy was a "handful," according to Lena. He once chased a cat into a dark closet and used a match to find him. As a result, the entire house burned to the ground, displacing his entire family. Sammy's father, Peter, was known to have a bad temper, according to Lena. Jimmy confirmed there was truth to Lena's recollection. We can make some excuses about why Peter Severino sometimes snapped. The poor man worked hard all day long, every day on the pig farm and had no time for leisure. One can surmise the stress of having to provide for a large family and to tend to a pig farm from sun up to sun down, day after day. This would cause any person to feel a high degree of stress. On October 31, 1928, Sammy left his house after having a physical altercation with his father. Perhaps he left to allow his dad time to cool off.

Night came and it was time to head home. The last thing Sammy did was grab on to the back of a moving trolley to hitch a ride home. Other family members recall it was the back of a bus. Whether it was a trolley or a bus, the result was the same. His grip failed and in a split second the boy lay bleeding in the road. Sammy's skull crushed on impact. He was thirteen years old. His cousin, Lena, remembers the funeral. She was a kid, too, and Sammy was not supposed to die. Sammy's mom, Nicoletta, cursed Halloween day from that point on. She and Peter, the father Sammy argued with, are also buried in St. Agnes Cemetery near their son. One has to wonder how Peter coped with the loss of his son given their last words were said in anger. Peter lived for forty-one more years, dying in 1969. He had a lot of time to think.

Sammy lies alone with a simple granite marker—his picture on a porcelain medallion centered on the stone. It is the only picture of him known to be in existence. His sweet face with large brown eyes and tussled dark hair show a child with all the promise of a long future. Sammy Serverino is gone but not forgotten.

Sammy Severino died in a traffic accident at age thirteen, but the story of his brief life came alive in the memories of his cousin and nephew.

The Day Three Lives Were Claimed:
The Orphans of St. Joseph's Industrial School

The lives of three young ladies were cut short one tragic afternoon in St. Agnes Cemetery. To this day it remains the saddest occurrence to happen on this sacred ground. The day was September 5, 1903—a late summer day of unusual warmth. The Sisters of Charity, entrusted with the care of the young women from the St. Joseph's Industrial School of Albany, brought them to Fernwood Pond located in a newly acquired area of the cemetery. According to a newspaper article in the St. Agnes Cemetery archives, fourteen girls, many attired in bathing suits, went into the pond to splash and frolic in the water to their heart's content. Parts of the pond were seventeen feet deep and as a precaution a fence was installed to separate the deep end from the shallow areas, which were no more than four feet deep. The fence did not prevent tragedy that day. Excerpts paraphrased from the news article bring us back to that day when Mary Breen, sixteen, Grace Burns, seventeen, and Mary O'Brien, twenty, drowned.

> *Someone had rigged up a light raft and on this the Misses Burns, O'Brien, Breen and 16-year-old Eva Layton were hugely enjoying themselves until they were suddenly precipitated into the water. They had ventured too far over the deep side of the fence. The terrified shrieks of the girls gave the first warning of danger. They were all struggling in the water—none of them could swim a stroke. The sisters fell to their knees and prayed and urged someone to save the girls. One classmate who could swim was dressed in long skirts but she bravely plunged into the pond without thinking of her own danger. Her skirts interfered with her and although she was near the girls she had to return to shore without having succeeded in saving them. The screams and cries for help attracted the attention of cemetery employees who rushed to their aid. They were helpless to do anything as only one man, Edwin McCann could swim. He saw four girls drowning before his eyes and plunged in. He*

The bodies of three young inmates of the St. Joseph's Industrial School were interred on September 8, 1903. They rested in unmarked graves for 107 years before they were properly memorialized with a stone donated anonymously.

MARY BREEN AGE 16

GRACE BURNS AGE 19

MARY O'BRIEN AGE 20

SEPT. 5, 1903

managed to reach the raft and holding on to it with one hand he grasped Eva Layton as she was sinking for the last time. The remaining three had gone down and there was nothing left to do but recover their bodies. The bottom of the pond gave up its dead nearly a half an hour later. The

Sisters of Charity were beside themselves with grief and could not be consoled.

Three small white caskets were carried out of St. Joseph's Industrial School on North Pearl Street at 9 a.m. on Tuesday, September 8, 1903. At least 1,000 people lined both sides of the street and sobs could be heard in every part of the neighborhood. Seldom is such a cortege seen on the streets of Albany and never before have three white hearses lined up at the same doorway to receive the bodies of three innocent young girls stricken down while in the bloom of womanhood. After a solemn mass held in St. Joseph's Church the three small caskets were brought to St. Agnes Cemetery and buried within a stone's throw from the scene of their doom.

The three girls were interred side by side in a lot donated by Rt. Rev. Bishop Burke. The grave remained unmarked until 2010, when a stone was donated and erected in their memory. On the back of the stone a sentence taken from the funeral sermon is inscribed, "God transplanted the sweet buds of their souls in paradise to bloom for an eternity."

GOD TRANSPLANTED THE SWEET BUDS
OF THEIR SOULS IN PARADISE TO BLOOM
FOR AN ETERNITY

◀◀ *Mary Breen, Grace Burns, and Mary O'Brien are gone but not forgotten. On the 107th anniversary of their death, Bishop Howard Hubbard blessed the newly installed headstone. The Daughters of Charity, the same order that was there on that fateful day, were in attendance.*

◀ *The grave of the three drowned girls remained unmarked until 2010, when this stone was donated and erected in their memory.*

61

CHAPTER 4

People in the Arts

Robert G. Vignola

I must confess that if not for a curious visitor to St. Agnes Cemetery, Menands, I would not have known we had a well-known Hollywood actor, screenwriter, and film director from the silent era to the 1930s buried here. Once rich and famous and now dead for more than six decades, Robert Vignola's name is again in the spotlight, albeit a humble light shed by the historian of an old, rural cemetery. No doubt he would have smiled at my ignorance. In his day, everyone knew his name. My visitor certainly knew and was extremely excited when I gave him a map to section nine, lot 86. I offered to take him up on site, telling him it would save him the time it will take for him to find the grave on his own. What I really wanted was to be enlightened about why having the remains of Robert G. Vignola resting in St. Agnes Cemetery was such a big deal!

Born on August 5, 1882, in Italy to Daniel and Rosa Vignola (buried in the same lot with him), Robert was raised in upstate New York. He relocated to Hollywood, California and began acting in silent films in the first decade of the 1900s before switching to a career in film directing. His career as a director brought him wealth and fame as evidenced by the beautiful Spanish-style home he lived in until his death on October 25, 1953. His last residence listed on his interment card is 6697 Whitley Terrance, Hollywood, California. A street view of this address on Google Earth is all you need for confirmation that the Italian American kid from upstate New York did OK for himself.

Among Vignola's many films to his credit are two big-budget epics, *When Knighthood Was in Flower* (1922) and a more well-known story titled *The Scarlet Letter* (1934). According to general information found on various Internet sites, Vignola's career as a director included 87 films, the first being a

The Vignola Family Lot in Section 9 is the only monument in St. Agnes Cemetery to feature an eighteenth-century-style skull-and-crossbones symbol. This type of symbol is Puritan in origin and does not reflect the Catholic Church's believe in the resurrection of the body. Under it are the words "is certain" [Death is Certain]. It is an interesting choice of iconography to place under the carved relief of Christ on the Cross.

DANIEL VIGNOLA
1845 — 1923

silent film in 1911. His life's accomplishments are significant to film historians, as I learned firsthand.

When I walk by Vignola's oversize granite pedestal tomb with vaulted roof I smile, and not only because I now know of his fame. The Vignola memorial is decorated with the image of a skull and crossbones more appropriate to early eighteenth-century Puritans. It is the only symbolism like it in the entire cemetery. It is not an approved religious symbol nor was it a popular funerary symbol after the early 1800s, making it a curious choice for a Catholic cemetery established in the Victorian era.

Close-up of the curious skull and crossbones iconography on the Vignola stone.

THESE SACRED GROUNDS

My Father the Artist

By Vincent J. Forte, Jr.

Vincent J. Forte, Sr. created his first public sculpture, the Sacred Heart of Jesus, for his father-in-law's headstone. Commissioned in 1959 by his mother-in-law, this was also his first use of granite.

Forte's other public works include a 1996 bronze bust of World War I hero Sergeant Henry Johnson, which is in Albany's Washington Park. It has become one of the city's iconic sculptures. Also in bronze is a 1992 bust of Christopher Columbus located in the Italian-American Community Center of Albany. There is a different bronze bust of Henry Johnson sculpted by Forte and completed posthumously by his son, Vincent Forte, Jr., which is in an Albany park dedicated to Sergeant Johnson. Located in the Chancery Office of the Catholic Diocese of Albany is Forte's 1978 mahogany deep relief of Bishop Howard J. Hubbard. At the time of his passing he was working on a commission for a marble bust of former President William Clinton.

Forte produced art skillfully in many mediums, including granite, marble, limestone, wood, oil painting, water color,

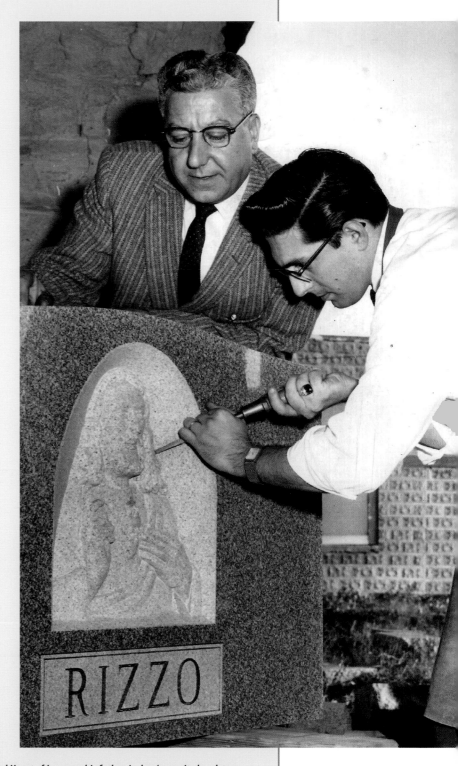

Vincent J. Forte, Sr. is pictured with his first public sculpture, the Sacred Heart of Jesus, on his father-in-law's granite headstone (now located in Saint Agnes Cemetery). Looking on is John Valente of Valente Memorials, Albany, New York, who loaned space and tools at his business for the project.

pastels, and pen and ink. He created music with the harmonica and tambourine, guitar, Hawaiian guitar, mandolin, and he loved to sing. Self-taught, he was never formally trained in art. His first artworks were completed before he entered kindergarten. Young Vincent used a straight pin to carve caricatures of prominent local people in school chalk brought home by his siblings.

Forte served in the U.S. Army during the Korean Conflict as a communications specialist and received two field promotions for his knowledge and leadership. After the war, he returned to Albany and worked as a civil and structural designer. Above all, his family was his most important passion, followed by art. He and his wife, Michelina, raised four children who went on to become engineers, an educator, and a designer. Each has also displayed in his or her own way, his artistic capabilities. A communicant of the Cathedral of the Immaculate Conception, he was known for his openness, generosity, and ability to let each person who met him feel special.

Vincent J. Forte, Sr. now rests in St. Agnes Mausoleum

First public sculpture completed by Vincent J. Forte, Sr.

THESE SACRED GROUNDS

Edward Hanlon enjoyed a prolific career in gravestone carving in the nineteenth century. He would be appalled at the current state of his own gravesite. It is slated for repair in the near future as funding permits. It is unclear if he carved his own monument. Most of his works are Gothic-style monoliths or die-on-base gravestones with decorative borders.

Mary Nash: Movie Star

Born in Troy, New York in 1884, Mary Nash (née Ryan) was a major film actress best known for her role as the cruel and conniving Fraulein Rottenmeir playing Shirley Temple's adversary in the 1937 film *Heidi*. Nash also appeared in a major role opposite Hollywood icons Cary Grant, James Stewart, and Katherine Hepburn in the 1940 film *The Philadelphia Story*, in which she played Hepburn's aristocratic mother. She remained in California throughout her career. She was married briefly to José Ruben in 1918 and is listed as "separated" when she died in her home on Sunset Boulevard on December 3, 1976. Her sister, Florence Nash, a lesser-known Hollywood actress, predeceased Mary in 1950.

Both girls got their start in Hollywood through their stepfather, Philip F. Nash, who was the second husband of their mother Ellen Frances Mack Ryan. Philip Nash had a long employment history in the theatrical business in New York City until his untimely death in 1914. Ellen, Philip, Florence, and Mary all rest in peace in the John Mack (Ellen's father) mausoleum. It is located at the end of a long line of classically designed private mausoleums that showcase the wealth and prosperity enjoyed by many of Albany's citizens of the Gilded Age and beyond.

◀ *Mary Nash began appearing in vaudeville as a dancer and then later in many off Broadway productions, including* Alice-Sit-by-the-Fire, *a 1905 production with Ethel Barrymore, and a 1915 play by George Bernard Shaw titled* Major Barbara. *She enjoyed a long and successful career on the big screen with some of the best and brightest stars.*

▶ *The final resting place for Mary Nash, who died at her home on Sunset Boulevard, Los Angeles, California in 1976 at the age of 92.*

St. Agnes Photography Contest

Between 2009 and 2013, St. Agnes Cemetery held a very popular photography contest. Local photographers were invited to submit photographs taken on cemetery grounds.

◀ *Private mausoleums on Mt. Olivet are timeless reflections of wealth, intellect, and impeccable taste. This photo won first place in the 2012 St. Agnes Cemetery photo contest.*

▶ *A winter sunset in St. Agnes Cemetery. This photo took first place in the 2011 cemetery photography contest.*

▲ *This photo won third place in the 2010 cemetery photo contest.*

◀ *This photo won second place in 2012.*

This photo of the Owen Golden Lot received an honorable mention in the 2013 cemetery photo contest.

Myron A. Cooney: A Man of Many Talents

Myron A. Cooney wrote the first and, until now, only book about St. Agnes Cemetery. It was published shortly before his death in 1898 at age 57. He was an accomplished man as noted in his obituary reprinted here:

Cooney—Myron A. Cooney, editor, critic playwright and musician, died June 21 at his residence in Albany, NY. Born in the city of Dublin, Ireland, on the 1st of March, 1811, he was a son of Myron Cooney, who was a very active of the Young Ireland organization, of which Smith O'Brien, Thomas Francis Meagher, Doheny and others were leaders. From his childhood his ruling passion was for study and music: and in the private schools of his native city he was fitted for college. His musical genius developed rapidly, and he was so diligent that before going to college he studied in the Royal Academy of Music, in London. In 1833 he entered the Catholic University of Dublin, where he applied to his studies with the closest attention and with all the enthusiasm of his youthful nature. He afterward studied in St. Patrick's College, Maynooth, leaving that institution at the end of his second year's divinity class. A marked feature of Mr. Cooney's intellectual characteristics was his intense love of modern languages. Ina comparatively short time he acquired a mastery of French, German and Italian. He came to this country in 1860. Turning his footsteps southward in search of some kind of work, he first secured a position as clerk on a Mississippi steamboat, in which capacity he acted until the war broke out. On returning to New York when the war was over he was placed on the staff of the New York Herald, and became the musical and dramatic editor of that paper. He wrote English librettos of the following operas: A Summer Night's Dream, Villars' Dragoons, The Chimes of Normandy, The Little Duke, The Two Cavaliers, Le Cid, Paul and Virginia, King of the Mountains, The Christian Martyr, The Beautiful Galetea, The Merry War, Apajune, *and many others. He moreover wrote a large number of vocal and instrumental works, some of which became highly popular, especially "The Nautilus Waltz," first brought out by Theodore*

This plain, simple stone does not reflect Myron Cooney's immense fame and fortune. He was a man of many talents—well known among elites in the music and literature community of the mid- to late nineteenth century.

Thomas, and of which 50,000 copies were sold while it was in the first flush of popularity. In January 1885, Mr. Cooney went to Albany, as editor-in-chief of the Argus, creditably filling that position until the fall of 1891, when he resigned. He was legislative correspondent of New York and Rochester papers during the session of 1892, and in June of that year became financial clerk of the State Department of Public Instruction—a responsible office, the duties of which he discharged with a great care, faithfulness and efficiency to the time of his last illness. His last musical composition, "St. Cecilia," a Roman drama, was produced by members of the Catholic Union of Albany under his personal direction a little over a year ago. As a newspaper writer, critic and dramatist, a man well versed in modern languages and literature, Myron A. Cooney had long occupied an honorable place among the cultivated men of the country.

CHAPTER 5

Civil War Stories

ST. AGNES CEMETERY IS THE FINAL RESTING PLACE of 525 Civil War soldiers identified to date. There are likely many more soldiers resting in the cemetery that have either unmarked stones or stones marked with a private memorial not denoting veteran status. In 2008, a volunteer-driven project to record the gravesites of known Civil War veterans and to assess the condition of their gravestones and markers was kicked off with a community meeting.

That year 250 soldiers and sailors were documented in a database. One of those volunteers was me, Kelly Grimaldi. I became a little obsessed with the project by my own admission. I knew there had to be many, many more men who served in the Civil War buried in this cemetery. Inch by inch I surveyed each section and each lot looking for the telltale sign of a white government-issued monolith that is easily recognizable as a veteran's gravestone. Well, the search would have been easy if the stones were not covered with a thick layer of sod—which at least 150 of them were. The remaining stones were broken and lying face down, obscuring the inscriptions.

A lot of excavation went on between 2008 and 2012. And then there were the unmarked veterans' graves I discovered after finding a survey of military graves completed in 1924. This valuable document was tucked away in a dusty old file deep in the cemetery's archives. It was pure gold to me, as it not only identified each veteran's name and regiment, but it also included the section and lot numbers so I could begin the process of obtaining marble monoliths for men who had never been memorialized. The project is ongoing and has involved descendants of Civil War soldiers and sailors wishing to ensure their veteran ancestors are properly memorialized.

Barney Ross: The Little Drummer Boy of a Different Sort

For young boys during the Civil War Era, war was not an abstract thought carefully orchestrated on the big screen or in play—it was real and it dominated their lives for four terrible years. All around them death hung in the air. There was no time to be young and carefree with death happening all around them. Cannons, muskets, bayonets, and disease became an inescapable reality for one young boy named Bernard Ross.

Bernard (Barney) Ross enlisted in the Third Infantry of the New York State Volunteer Army on April 19, 1861, to serve two years. He was only twelve years old when he joined his regiment as a drummer boy. Too young and small (the muster roll indicates he was only four feet ten inches tall) he was charged with the task of keeping the beat of his drum in time with the march of heavy boots belonging to men who were not a whole lot older than him. It is not clear to me why his parents would let their firstborn son enlist in the army at age twelve, but I suspect it had to do with the small stipend that he would earn for his service. His parents, Simon and Mary Ross, had seven other mouths to feed and for a poor Irish immigrant family, Barney's small stipend could have made the difference between eating and starving. Barney, by modern standards, would have been a seventh grader—just an innocent child marching off to war.

Photograph of Barney Ross contributed by Laura LaDuke.

Before he could be discharged in May 1863, Barney witnessed the death of 122 men in his company alone. Instead of returning home when given the opportunity, he reenlisted for another three-year term. He saw intense action in Morris Island, South Carolina and against Fort Sumter and Charleston before marching straight into the hell of Cold Harbor and eventually into trench warfare in Petersburg. It was during the siege of Petersburg, on July 3, 1864, that disease silenced his drum and

confined him to a hospital bed where he lay suffering from a fever that nearly claimed his life. The relatively harmless war games played by today's twelve-year-olds are a far cry from the action Barney saw. Blood-soaked uniforms, gaping wounds, and agonizing screams of pain were not entertainment on a movie screen—these things were Barney's reality.

Not much is known about this child after he returned to his family's home in Albany in late 1864. Census data of 1880 finds Barney, age 33, unmarried and still living at home with his aging parents. Six years later he was dead. His grave in historic St. Agnes Cemetery is marked with a deteriorated marble stone that has fallen over and is barely legible. It is among the hundreds of gravesites for Civil War veterans that are in the process of being restored. It is the very least we can do for the little drummer boy who served the Union cause. And while the Civil War did not take Bernard Ross's life, one can assume that the twelve-year-old boy who left home on April 19, 1861, never really returned. We will never know the extent of the physical or psychological damage the war had on Barney. His innocence must have faded like the sound of his drum among the firing of cannon and the screams of the dying.

John McElveney: Too Old to Serve, Too Young to Die

Today our country may be hard pressed to find a 49-year-old family man eager to join a volunteer army and plunge himself into war. But Irish immigrant John McElveney was so keen to defend the Union cause during the Civil War that he lied about his age and enlisted in Company E of the Sixty-third Regiment, New York State Volunteer Army—the "Irish Brigade." He had to have known the danger he put himself in when he purposely deceived the enlistment officer and shaved five years off his age to qualify for military service. He enlisted on January 4, 1864, and by that time thousands of New Yorkers were dead, missing, or severely wounded.

This marble stone for Bernard Ross replaced the original stone dated 1886. More than 100 Civil War veterans in St. Agnes Cemetery have new stones marking their graves. Marble does not hold up well in the New York State climate. A grassroots effort began in 2007 to survey the cemetery, record all Civil War veterans' gravesites, and complete a condition assessment of each gravestone. Broken and illegible stones were replaced with marble reproductions.

Entire communities were bound together in a perpetual state of mourning. Widows and orphans struggled to survive—many having to depend on the charity of strangers or alms from their church. Despite what was at stake, Private John McElveney left his home in the dead of winter to join his much younger comrades for a march into hell.

John's oldest son Daniel, also a native of Ireland, was among those who waved good-bye that cold January day. Six months after John enlisted he was wounded at Petersburg and transported to a hospital in Alexandria, Virginia until death finally relieved his agony on September 7, 1864. Private John McElveney was hastily buried in a makeshift cemetery near the hospital. No family members were present and no tears were shed upon his grave. Like many thousands of his fellow New Yorkers, John fought for the Union and ultimately gave his life for a cause he passionately believed in—the preservation of a united nation. His son Daniel, assumed the role of patriarch. He eventually opened a large, double-front store which he owned, where he manufactured candies and fine confectionary, ice cream and quality cakes located at 97 South Pearl Street, Albany, NY. Daniel owned a second store on North Pearl Street as well. He is described as a gentleman, pleasant and agreeable in his manners, and retained an excellent reputation as a successful and honest businessman his entire life. And he never, ever forgot his father's great sacrifice.

THESE SACRED GROUNDS

◀ The McElveney Family lot features an impressive granite monument standing at least sixteen feet high. The large Latin cross is seen propped up against the stone foundation. Crosses often fall from the top of monuments because the iron pin holding it in place gets rusty and weak. The result is a large collection of crosses at rest on the ground.

▶ Thought to be Saint Catherine of Siena, the Martineau monument features a statue made of nonferrous metal resembling stone. It is unique in this cemetery full of marble, granite, and sandstone carvings.

J. FRANK ZUMBO
KILLED IN KOREA
AUG 2 1953

Thirteen years after his father's death, Daniel arranged for the disinterment of John's remains and had them transported home for a decent Christian burial in St. Agnes Cemetery, Menands. The soldier's grave, once marked with only a simple wooden cross in a sad little Virginian cemetery, is now memorialized with a beautifully carved granite obelisk that is twenty feet tall. Daniel's grand gesture spoke of his love and admiration for a father who fought and died for their adopted country.

Recently the great-great-great granddaughter of Private John McElveney came to St. Agnes Cemetery in Menands to inquire about the "Adopt a Civil War Veteran" project. Realizing how fortunate her ancestor was to have been returned home to be buried in the family lot and memorialized in such a grand manner, she decided to "adopt" the grave of a less fortunate soldier who had served in the same company and regiment as Private McElveney. Thanks to the generosity of a stranger, Private Michael Hickey received

▲ *The McElveneys owned a popular cake shop in Albany shown here.*

◄ *This classical angel is a touching memorial to a young soldier killed in action in the Korean War.*

a proper memorial in honor of his service to his country. We will never know if John and Michael came to know each other well as they marched together in strange lands wondering if they would survive the day. The important thing is, even after 150 years, neither soldier has been forgotten. Both rest peacefully in a beautiful, historic cemetery where the living keep the memory of the dead alive through kind deeds like the one Eileen Dulin Richardson bestowed upon Private Hickey. John is no doubt is smiling down upon his great, great, great granddaughter with tremendous pride.

Honoring a Young Soldier's Memory

Many men killed on the battlefield during the Civil War were buried where they lay. This left families without any sense of closure. Such was the case with Arthur O'Keeffe. In 2012, Elizabeth Fiore, a distant relative of Corporal O'Keeffe asked that we mark the grave with a cenotaph—a memorial in memory of someone not buried at the site. This soldier, who was 21 when he was killed, will now never be forgotten.

Here is the letter Arthur O'Keeffe's family received from the Union Army, notifying them of his death:

A portrait of Corporal Arthur O'Keeffe.

Hqrs, Co. B, 34th Regt
Camp near Falmouth, VA.
Dec. 30, 1862

Mr. Michael O'Keeffe,

Sir,

I am sorry to have to be obliged to pen the sorrowful news to you of your estimable sons misfortune. The circumstances are as follows. On the 17th of Sept. 1862 your son went with me into the Battle of Sharpsburg, Md. & then and there he received a severe wound & I told him to fall back to the rear out of danger as soon as he could and since that time I have neither seen or heard from him. In all probability he died from the effects of his wound and had been buried on the Battle field. I here inform you that your son was a good and brave soldier and a kind companion. I assure you I fully appreciate your loss of so noble a son who willingly laid down his life for the Restoration of our Noble Banner. Enclosed you find his descriptive list which will enable you to collect his back pay & bounty. Please let me know if you receive this and by so doing you will oblige.

Orrin W. Beach, 2nd Lieut.
Commanding, Co. B
34th Regt. N.Y.S.V.
Washington, D.C.

In 2012, a distant relative of Corporal O'Keeffe asked St. Agnes to mark the grave with a cenotaph—a memorial in memory of someone not buried at the site.

IN MEMORY OF
ARTHUR A O'KEEFFE
CORP CO B E
34 NY INF

OCT 18 1840
SEP 17 1862
KILLED AT
ANTIETAM

Draped urns are a symbol for mourning. This one is decorated with ivy—a symbol of love and friendship.

88

Jeremiah Stokes: A "Galvanized Yankee" in St. Agnes Cemetery

By Joseph F. Meany, great-grandson of Jeremiah Stokes

Jeremiah Stokes was a "Galvanized Yankee" during and after the American Civil War. The term has a touch of Western humor because when an electric current is passed through a tin cup, for example, its color changes from grayish to, sort of, bluish. Since "Galvanized Yankees" were Union soldiers recruited from among Confederate prisoners-of-war, Westerners who encountered them thought the term appropriate. The ex-rebs do not seem to have taken offense. In all, nearly six thousand foreign-born Confederate prisoners—enough to form six full-strength infantry regiments—elected to take the oath to the United States and join the Union Army. They were not asked to fight their former colleagues in gray. They would be sent west to replace the frontier regulars now fighting the Civil War.

The year was 1864. General Grant had canceled the policy of exchanging prisoners. Why fight the same men twice, he reasoned? Because of this, large prisoner-of-war camps were built at Elmira, New York; Sandusky, Ohio; and Rock Island, Illinois to hold the incarcerated rebels. The new prison camps contained many foreign-born prisoners who might very well be willing to trade gray uniforms for blue and a chance to get out of prison. In October 1864, President Lincoln sent his military aide, Captain Henry Rathbone (the man who would be beside the president in Ford's Theater the next April) to Rock Island to begin recruiting from among the foreign-born rebels held on the barren island in the upper Mississippi River. One of the Confederate prisoners who agreed to enlist was Jeremiah Stokes.

His service record shows Jeremiah enlisting in the Confederate Army on August 27, 1862, five days before the Confederate Conscription Act took effect. For enlisting, he received a bounty of $50 "confederate." Jeremiah served in Company B, Sixty-third Georgia Infantry until June 1863, when he is described first as "Absent With Leave," and then "Absent Without Leave," and then as "Deserted." By deserting, he contrived to miss the Battle of Fort Wagner, in Charleston Harbor, one of the bloodiest actions of the war. For six months, he remained a fugitive. Then, in February 1864, he is described as "Present In Arrest." At the end of his sentence in the cells at Fort Jackson, Jeremiah was returned to duty. The Civil War was about to catch up with Private Jeremiah Stokes.

In May 1864, General Sherman was poised to move south into Georgia. His objective: the rebel rail and industrial center at Atlanta. Confederate reinforcements were scraped together from garrison troops guarding the Atlantic coast. The Sixty-third Georgia was ordered to report to General Joseph E. Johnston's Army of Tennessee at Dalton, Georgia. Jeremiah was about to experience a new element of modern warfare: the strategic movement of troops by rail.

Viewed at the macro level, the Atlanta campaign lends itself to those chess and fencing metaphors so often used by historians to describe military operations. But on the micro level, the reality was anything but an antiseptic chessboard. The reality was a series of exhausting marches and countermarches, usually at night and often in torrential rain. It meant soaked clothing that never dried, sleepless nights, mud, and paralyzing terror of death or dismemberment. And overall, the numbing knowledge of being greatly outnumbered, outclassed in resources of every kind, and overwhelmed by a relentless federal juggernaut. Even those committed to the cause realized that resistance was futile and defeat inevitable.

The back of the stone marking the grave of Jeremiah Stokes, his wife, and son.

Jeremiah's shooting war lasted six weeks, from the opening of the campaign in May 1864 until he was captured in mid-June. The Sixty-third Georgia was first in reserve in Crow Creek Valley behind a feature called "Buzzard's Roost." There, on May 6, 1864, Jeremiah was in action for the first time. There he first experienced the crescendo of musketry, the banshee scream of artillery projectiles, and the stream of maimed, confused, and wounded men making for the rear. There he saw his first corpse lying in the road.

The Sixty-third retreated in a series of night marches, from Crow Valley to Dug Gap and from Dug Gap across the Oostanula River to Calhoun. No sooner had

The front of the stone marking the grave of Jeremiah Stokes, his wife, and son.

they arrived than they were ordered back across the river and up to Tilton Station, on the railroad halfway back to Dalton. Reaching Tilton Station their orders were again changed and they countermarched back to Calhoun.

The Federals had thrown a division, Sweeney's, across the Oostanula at Lay's Ferry. The Confederate troops at Calhoun were the only force available to contest the crossing. Exhausted, the Sixty-third Georgia was roused and thrown into battle. At Lay's Ferry, Jeremiah faced the enemy directly. This enemy proved to be tough, holding the bridgehead until reinforced, and then driving the Confederates from the field. Jeremiah's first pitched battle was a defeat, the experience both terrifying and disheartening.

General Johnston ordered a night withdrawal intended to break contact and shorten and consolidate his line. Of all tactical evolutions, a night withdrawal offers the most probability of confusion, and in the confusion Jeremiah either got lost, or more likely, slipped away deliberately. It was an extraordinarily dangerous undertaking, to surrender to those hardened union skirmishers as they warily advanced through the woods, anticipating contact at any moment, and primed to shoot first and ask questions afterward. But by some miracle the Yankees held their fire and made Jeremiah a prisoner.

Jeremiah was marched to the POW collection point at Acworth, Georgia. Acworth was General Sherman's railhead. In locked freight cars, Jeremiah and his fellow prisoners began the long trip north. By July 1864, Jeremiah and the other prisoners were languishing on starvation rations, imposed in deliberate reprisal for conditions at Andersonville and other southern prisons. On Rock Island, the prisoners were reduced to eating rats, cats, and, on one special occasion, the sutler's dog. The psychological effects on survivors of the Irish famine can only be imagined.

While Jeremiah and his fellows struggled to survive the hunger, malnutrition, and the increasing cold, events were playing out in the West that would have a profound influence on his life. On November 29, 1864, Col. John M. Chivington's Third Colorado Cavalry attacked the peaceful camp of Black Kettle's Cheyennes on Sand Creek, thirty miles from Fort Lyon, Colorado Territory. The Sand Creek Massacre only inflamed the Native Americans' will to resist. General John Pope, commanding the Military Division of the Missouri, braced for "a bloody year on the plains." Pope was desperate for reinforcements and bombarded his superiors with pleas for more troops. He had to have them in place by spring when the prairie grass was tall enough to support Native American ponies and when the winter camps scattered into highly mobile war parties.

What Pope needed were foot soldiers. The Order of Battle, dated December 31, 1864, reveals that Pope did not have a single infantry soldier in the District of the Upper Arkansas. Reinforcements were available from a new and unorthodox manpower pool. Nearly six thousand volunteers had been recruited in the fall of 1864 from among the thousands of rebel prisoners collecting in federal camps. The program was open to foreign-born enlisted Confederates willing to take the Oath of Allegiance to the United States. Promised they would not be used against the south, they were available to be sent west to the wars vs. Native Americans. Among those who accepted the government's offer was a twenty-four-year-old Irish-born Confederate prisoner named Jeremiah Stokes. He headed west and deep into Native American country. Lieutenant Colonel King assumed command issuing "Instructions to Officers Commanding Escorts" in which he succinctly synthesized the tactical problem of Indian warfare: "Never imagine because you do not see any Indians . . . that there are none in your neighborhood."

On April 9, Lee surrendered in far-off Virginia. Five days later, President Lincoln was assassinated at Ford's Theater in Washington. The news reached Fort Riley on April 17. Jeremiah probably heard the news a few days later. By autumn 1865, hostilities were concluded and regulars were arriving from the East. The volunteers, with the Civil War now over for six months, clamored for release. On October 10, General Pope requested authority to reenlist men from the Second and Third "Galvanized Yankees." He described his state troops as "dissatisfied and mutinous" while his former rebs were "good soldiers in good discipline." Grant refused the request. On November 7, 1865, Jeremiah received his full pay and mustered out of federal service. The regiment disbanded.

Before he was twenty-five, Jeremiah had survived the Irish famine and service in both the Confederate and Union armies. Finally settling in Albany, New York, he purchased a grave lot in St. Agnes Cemetery. When he died in 1915, he was buried there, later joined by his wife and son and daughter. To paraphrase the old music hall tune, "He'd come a long way from Tipperary."

Remembering Our Veterans

We must never forget our veterans. St. Agnes Cemetery is the final resting place for thousands of men and women who served in times of peace and times of war, from the American Civil War to present conflicts in the Middle East.

Three men were awarded the Congressional Medal of Honor for their valor. Captain Patrick White was cited for his role in the Battle of Vicksburg of 1863. He and his men carried a cannon by hand up a hill and fired it through Confederate lines, thus saving thousands of Union soldiers from an almost certain death.

Private Frank Fournia put his own life on the line when he rushed into the middle of a gun battle to save his wounded comrades during the Spanish American War. Private First Class Parker Dunn, three times rejected for service by the Army because of his eyesight and frail stature, was finally accepted into service in 1918. While on active duty in France on October 18, he selflessly embarked on a suicide mission to get a message to troops unwittingly in the path of an encroaching enemy. Though he suffered three gunshot wounds in the process, the last being ultimately fatal, his mission was successful. The Dunn Memorial Bridge in Albany is named for him.

◀ *Three Congressional Medal of Honor recipients are buried in St. Agnes.*

▶ *Sometimes mistaken as a symbol of service in the Navy, the anchor is actually the symbol for hope. Here it is found on a barely legible marble stone dating from the 1860s.*

The Padula family monument is one of the most photographed monuments in the cemetery. It features a life-size sculpture of the Pieta, which faces the rising sun.

CHAPTER 6

Captains of Industry

 Anthony Nicholas Brady: Midas Man of the Gilded Era

Everything Anthony Brady touched turned to gold. In his lifetime, he amassed such a fortune he was known as one of the wealthiest men in the world. His enormous private mausoleum designed in the style of the Greek Parthenon is valued today at nearly $4 million. He is described as a shrewd and brilliant businessman. He was one of the first businessmen to capitalize on the invention of electricity, having locked in a contract in 1881 to light the streets of Albany. (He seemed to be ahead of every cutting edge modern invention.)

Brady was a generous man and well known for his philanthropy. He founded the Brady Maternity Hospital in Albany because of his deep concern for the well-being of mothers and babies. His hospital opened two years after his death and served hundreds of thousands of families until it closed in the late 1960s.

Brady died on July 23, 1913, at age 71 of an acute gastric attack while in London. It is said at the time of his death he was still grief-stricken by

Anthony Nicholas Brady's family mausoleum is an elaborate granite tomb with a beautiful stained glass window. Many of the mausoleums in St. Agnes Cemetery reflect Greek and Roman revival influences. Through this architectural style we see the philosophical and artistic contributions our departed citizens gave to the aesthetics of St. Agnes Cemetery. Classically styled private mausoleums do more than house the dead. They are testimony to the appreciation people had for history, perfection, and beauty. The Brady mausoleum, built in 1912, resembles the Greek Parthenon, 447–438 B.C.

the death of his daughter, Flora, who was killed with three sisters of the Hamilton family when the train car they were riding in derailed and crashed into the engine, burning them alive. Flora Brady Gavit was the first to be interred in the large family mausoleum. Brady was well respected, a good Catholic, and a good husband and father. He will never be forgotten.

◀ *Flora Brady was killed in a fiery train wreck along with three Hamilton sisters. It was a devastating loss to two prominent Albany families. Her final resting place is seen here inside the Brady Mausoleum.*

▲ *The Brady Mausoleum is perfectly symmetrical with fluted Doric order columns and a classic portico with an unadorned pediment. Its interior is lined in white marble.*

▶ *Anthony Brady was a generous man of the highest order. Right before his death in 1913, Brady gave the Roman Catholic Diocese of Albany enough money to build a maternity hospital on North Main Avenue in Albany (now the main office for the Diocese). Nearly 100,000 babies were born in the hospital from its opening in 1915 until it closed in 1969. Sadly, hundreds of babies died or were stillborn. Their tiny bodies rest in Section 2 in a large lot donated by the Brady family. The graves are unmarked except for this modest slant granite memorial that receives countless visitors all year long. Rest in peace sweet angels in heaven.*

◀ *Stained glass window in the Brady Mausoleum restored in 2016 by Chapman Stained Glass, Inc. of Albany, NY.*

▶ *The Bette Family monument was installed in 2014 in honor of Michael Bette, patriarch of the well-known Bette & Cring Construction Group, who died in 2013. Mr. Bette, a devoted Catholic and generous benefactor to the Albany Diocese, rests surrounded by other captains of industry and supporters of the Catholic Church. This monument's style and size harken back to the Gilded Era of monumentalism. The Celtic cross at the top appears to be basking in the light of heaven.*

In the Style of the High Renaissance

Notes of classicism are found in the stained-glass windows of private mausoleums. This is the interior of the Walsh Mausoleum built in the 1930s. While many families of that era were choosing to build in the style of Art Deco, William Edward Walsh's final resting place features many stylistic elements of the High Renaissance. The structure's exterior features fluted, Ionic order columns supporting a portico with a parapet more consistent with Spanish Mission architecture than Greco Roman classicism. The Walsh family owned W. E. Walsh & Sons' Department Store on State Street in Albany. The store catered to a wealthy clientele. Mr. Walsh started out making hats—some of the very finest known in the area. He built an empire and his final resting place reflects his success.

High Renaissance-style stained-glass windows adorn the Walsh family mausoleum.

THESE SACRED GROUNDS

This highly detailed bronze door on the Walsh family mausoleum features both biomorphic and zoomorphic motifs interwoven within a pattern of rhythmic lines. It is decorative and functional, securing the crypts lining the inside walls.

Rags to Riches

Nicholas Thomas Kane lived a rags to riches story. Born in Ireland, his family immigrated to the United States in 1848. They settled in Albany when he was just two years old. Kane served in the Union Army, joining the 20th New York Cavalry in 1863 and was mustered out in 1865 as a private.

After the war, he and several of his relatives worked in woolen mills in New York and Rhode Island. It is unclear how he pulled himself out of poverty to become a wealthy owner of several productive mills in New York, but indeed he did. He died at age 39 after being elected a New York State congressman but before he could assume office.

The newspaper article below gives a sense of Kane's sterling reputation at the time of his death.

Nicholas Thomas Kane's elaborate monument features the only free standing bronze bust in the cemetery.

Congressman Kane Dying
ALBANY, N.Y., SEPTEMBER 2, 1887

Congressman-elect Nicholas T. Kane, of the Albany district, lies in a dying condition at his home in West Troy. His physicians have announced that his condition is hopeless, and his death is expected at any hour. He has not been well since his election, and most of his time since then has been devoted toward regaining his health. He has been gradually wasting away from the effects of that dread disease, consumption. Mr. Kane has had a remarkable business career. Eight or nine years ago he was working by the day in a woolen mill in Washington County. He then branched out in business for himself and leased a knitting mill, and is estimated to have become worth in that short time upward of a quarter of a million dollars. He is a man of great personal popularity and defeated Dr. Swinburne in the Congressional contest last fall.

Grace Reavy: A Woman of Substance

Grace Reavy was born in 1877. The State of New York in 1877 was still a patriarchal society that held on to the idea that women had no place in politics or public office of any kind. Reavy, the daughter of an undertaker from Cohoes, New York, was the first woman in New York to break through that glass ceiling when she was appointed by Cohoes's mayor, Michael Foley, to serve as Cohoes City Comptroller in 1919. It was the first time in New York history a woman held a municipal public office.

▲ *Photograph of Grace Reavy.*

▼ *Grace Reavy's family monument.*

Her career did not end there. She successfully pursued a career in public service and was appointed to several respectable positions, including Cohoes City Treasurer, Commissioner of Elections, and Deputy Secretary of State in Franklin D. Roosevelt's first term as governor of New York. Never blinded by her own ambition, Reavy was a dutiful public servant who advocated for years on behalf of women's rights issues.

She and Eleanor Roosevelt became friends and together they were a force to be reckoned with in their mission to advance women's opportunities in the workplace and in public office.

She seemingly never tired. She was in her late seventies when she was named to the Albany County Board of Health. Her commitment to a variety of worthy causes continued until her death at nearly eighty-two years old in 1959. Grace Reavy's legacy as a woman of substance lives on though she herself rests in peace in St. Agnes Cemetery.

John H. Farrell: Founder of the *Times Union* Newspaper

Portions of this text were excerpted from Amasa Parker's Landmarks of Albany Co.

John Henry Farrell was born Sept. 1, 1839 on the southern outskirts of Albany at Abbey Farm. He worked on his family's acreage growing up. While attending Christian Brothers Academy, Farrell landed a part-time job under editor Hugh Hastings, an Irish immigrant who ascended local newspaper ranks to run the *Albany Knickerbocker*. At 16, he became an apprentice printer to Luther Tucker, powerful publisher of the popular *Cultivator and Country Gentleman*. By the age of 19, Farrell had worked his way up from inky printer to the cleaner and more lucrative job of editor of the telegraph news for the Albany papers connected with the Associated Press. Disseminating news by telegraph was still a slow, labor-intensive business during Farrell's time. The biggest story for newspapermen, and the nation, in this era and for generations to come was the Civil War. The telegraph was a vital link for allowing news from the battlegrounds to reach readers of the Albany newspapers, which lacked the resources and staff to send their own correspondents to the front.

The Civil War dragged on for long, troubling years. For Farrell, the telegraph editor, the news never stopped pouring in and he worked grueling hours. While editing the AP telegraph dispatches, Farrell freelanced pieces for the city's dominant dailies, *The Argus* and *Evening Journal*. Working his contacts paid off and he was offered the job as city editor of *The Argus*. After just four months as city editor of the Argus, Farrell was put in charge of launching that paper's new Sunday edition, *The Sunday Press*. One year later, in the summer of 1871, he was running this new Sunday entity.

Still in his thirties, Farrell teamed with older, more experienced editors Myron Rooker and James Macfarlane to purchase *The Daily Press* and *The Knickerbocker* and merged the two in 1878. Farrell and his partners ran the paper profitably for two decades until Farrell decided to sell off his interest in March 1891 for $50,000 cash, roughly $1.5 million in today's dollars. Farrell and his wife, Mary, had reared seven children, and after the newspaper sale, the couple settled quietly in their large brownstone across from Washington Park in Albany, New York.

Simple granite steps inscribed with the name "John H. Farrell" lead up to small, plain granite stones marking the graves of Farrell family members. The grave lot is understated and in no way reflects the immense wealth John Farrell accumulated during his lifetime.

After four months of idleness, Farrell, bored and itching to get back into the newspaper fray, purchased three small, struggling papers in the summer of 1891: *The Evening Union*, *Evening Times*, and *Albany Sun*. At the same time, Farrell bought property on the corner of Beaver and Green streets, remodeled an industrial brick building and made it his newspaper plant. Farrell ushered a newly minted newspaper into the modern era. The *Times Union* was born. He was also a former trustee of St. Agnes Cemetery. He died on April 13, 1894.

John McArdle: Devoted to Orphans in Life and Death

John McArdle was a very popular tavern owner in Albany in his day. He made a comfortable life for himself and amassed great wealth before dying in 1874 at the age of sixty. McArdle was one of the original trustees for St. Agnes Cemetery. The lot he chose is the largest in the cemetery. It sits high upon Founders' Hill and is encircled by bronze reliefs set in ornately carved granite depicting Christ's journey to Calvary.

Large bronze statues of the Virgin Mary and St. John the Baptist flank the center entrance. Generous beyond compare, McArdle donated one-third of his cemetery lot to the Daughters of Charity who ran St. Vincent's Orphanage. He donated the equivalent of $300,000 in today's money to the orphanage and gave of his time to the children. The remaining third of his lot was set aside for the burial of orphaned children.

John McArdle was one of the original trustees of St. Agnes. The statues and monument adorning his plot, shown here, occupy the largest lot in the cemetery.

A late October snow dusts St. Agnes Cemetery with the promise of more to come.

DESMOND

Large bronze statues of the Virgin Mary and St. John the Baptist flank the center entrance of the resting place of John McArdle, a very popular tavern owner in Albany in his day and one of the original trustees for St. Agnes Cemetery.

Thomas Cantwell: Expert in Fighting Forgery

Thomas Cantwell's gravestone is simple, but his complex, industrious life was not. Born in Albany in May 1845, Cantwell was active in politics, the newspaper business, and the banking business. He was best known as a skillful expert in the detection of fraudulent bank bills. He served the government by lending his expertise in counterfeit cases. Cantwell's services were in high demand across the country as a judge of forgeries of signatures and handwriting in general.

He was also very involved in helping to bust what was dubbed The Canal Ring—a group of corrupt contractors and politicians who conspired to defraud New York State by overbilling for work done on the state's canal system. Thomas Cantwell, a man of great integrity until his death in 1914, served as a Trustee of St. Agnes Cemetery.

Gravestone of Thomas Cantwell.

CHAPTER 7

Modern Burial Trends

ONE HUNDRED AND FIFTY YEARS AFTER ITS CONSECRATION, St. Agnes Cemetery is still actively serving Catholic families. The landscape of Catholic burial has changed over the years, and St. Agnes Cemetery has changed with it. You can see the changes as you travel south from Founders Hill. The elaborate Victorian lots give way to smaller family lots, then to the shrine sections, community mausoleums, and urn gardens.

Today, the cemetery offers a full range of burial options. Traditional family lots, with an upright granite monument, remain the choice of many. Others prefer shrine sections, first developed in the 1950s, which feature a central statue surrounded by individual graves memorialized with bronze markers.

Private family mausoleums have never really gone out of style. These granite structures offer enduring beauty and architectural integrity, often customized with personal touches to fulfill the vision and wishes of the family.

St. Agnes has two community mausoleums, St. Agnes Mausoleum and American Saints Mausoleum. These buildings feature both interior and exterior crypts, polished granite and marble, and original artwork.

American Saints Mausoleum, built in 2002, features beautiful wood carved icons and bronze reliefs of the Stations of the Cross.

◀ *Inside St. Agnes Mausoleum, built in 1987.*

▼ *Two sections in the cemetery are reserved for the burial of cremated remains of people who donated their bodies to the Anatomical Gift Program through Albany Medical College. Graves may be marked with a bronze vase. Every September, Albany Diocesan Cemeteries offers a special memorial service at which family and medical students pay their respects to the people who made the ultimate gift to the study of medicine.*

Lawn crypts are another recent innovation. These pre-installed double depth concrete vaults conserve space and are less costly for consumers.

Cremation was unknown in America when St. Agnes was consecrated. In fact, the Church prohibited cremation until 1963. To accommodate Church teaching that the remains of cremated bodies should be buried or entombed, St. Agnes has developed urn gardens, columbariums, and niches in community mausoleums.

Albany Diocesan Cemeteries continues to seek innovative ways to keep St. Agnes Cemetery relevant for future generations of Catholics.

▲ *Glass niches in American Saints Mausoleum provide an alternative to traditional niches. These niches allow families to memorialize their loved ones in beautiful urns visible to all. Some families include a photo of the deceased.*

▶ *View from St. Teresa's Shrine facing east. The Menands Bridge is seen in the background. Private family mausoleums along the road show yet another final resting place choice offered in Historic St. Agnes Cemetery.*

THESE SACRED GROUNDS

▶ *The quiet of an early morning mist over St. Teresa's Shrine section decorated with Christmas wreaths and blankets.*

▲ *This weeping cherry tree was planted in memory of Patricia Russo who suffered an untimely death in 2007. Her devoted and devastated husband, James Russo, would visit the cemetery a few times a week and place flowers by her niche in American Saints Mausoleum and by this tree. He was a dear man and a generous supporter of the cemetery. Mr. Russo used to worry what would happen to the tree after he died. Our staff promised him they would keep it pruned and watered. His tree comes alive with blossoms early in the spring. It was in full bloom when he died on May 6, 2013. He never got to see it. We are taking care of your tree Mr. Russo—just as we promised. Rest in peace.*

▲ *Memorial butterflies are a beautiful way to honor the memory of a loved one. These lovely bronze butterflies are securely mounted on an outside wall of the American Saints Mausoleum.*

THESE SACRED GROUNDS

Unlike the ostentatious Victorians of the Gilded Era, most people these days are not purchasing enormous grave lots and erecting 20-foot monuments to memorialize themselves and their family. Of course, it is a matter of money and priorities. Victorians thought it very important to ensure there was no question of their individual social status in life. The grander the monument the grander the ladies and gentlemen's bones will be perceived for all time. No shame in that because that line of thinking gave us remarkable grave lots in which to feast our eyes on in Historic St. Agnes Cemetery. However, there is a downside. Cemeteries with many different size monuments condensed on uneven ground are difficult to maintain. Mowers and trimmers damage monuments and hills make navigation of mowing machines difficult. In response to that issue, lawn park-style cemeteries featuring even ground and flat, uniformly placed grave markers in a grid-like pattern became all the rage in the 1950s. They were established to be easier to maintain and to be more cost effective. They also conserve

◄ *St. Teresa shrine statue marking one of four shrine sections in the cemetery.*

▲ *St. Agnes Community Mausoleum juxtaposed with old marble stones in the middle and St. Joseph's Shrine Section in the foreground. Three very different burial practices span nearly 200 years of history.*

ground for more burials because there are no monuments to take up space. In St. Agnes Cemetery, the modern concept of a lawn park cemetery is employed in four large sections: Queen of Heaven Shrine, Sacred Heart Shrine, St. Teresa's Shrine, and St. Joseph's Shrine. Bronze markers mounted on granite foundations serve as respectable memorials.

◄ *Monuments of the Victorian era were designed to comfort the living. They are often sentimental, like this one of a woman—possibly a saint—looking down lovingly and peacefully at the small child clinging to her skirts. This type of funerary art is in stark contrast to the frightening skulls and skeletons found on gravestones of the eighteenth century.*

► *A perfect example of a Victorian-era monument is the beautiful Thacher Angel, designed and carved by artist genius Carl Conrads for two-year-old Gabrielle Thacher Morris. The beloved little girl died of meningitis on September 15, 1894. Children died with unfortunate regularity in the nineteenth century and most were not memorialized in such a grand manner, making the Thacher Angel something to behold both for its design and its sentiment. Though little Gabrielle's father was a physician, he was unable to stop the ravages of bacterial meningitis. An estimated 25 percent of children in the nineteenth century died before their fifth birthday. Rest in peace little Gabby.*

Seemingly deep in thought, this figure carved in marble on top of the granite pedestal of the Palladino family monument holds a laurel wreath symbolic of victory in death. The symbolism dates back to ancient Rome, when winners of contests were crowned with a laurel wreath meant to bestow upon the triumphant a promise of immortality. The hope of a joyful resurrection gives the living a measure of peace.

130

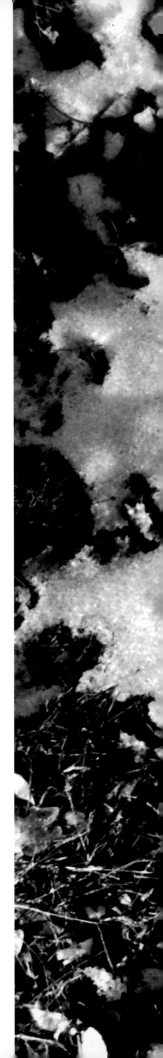

Restoring and Preserving St. Agnes Cemetery for the Ages

IN 2008, A COMPREHENSIVE SURVEY and gravestone assessment project was conducted on the cemetery's grounds. Monuments considered to be of historical significance were prioritized and an annual fundraiser was planned to raise money for their restoration. Eight years later and many hundreds of monuments and a few mausoleums later, we see a remarkable transformation of our oldest sections. Marble and granite stones—some enormous in size and elaborate in design—were strapped and hoisted off the ground, cleaned and pieced back together. Smaller stones were not ignored. Hundreds were dug out of the ground, pieced together using best practices defined by the respected Association for Gravestone Studies, and lined up in neat, orderly rows as was the original intent. Cemetery staff and volunteers did what they could to pitch in. It is amazing how many people gathered here over the years to lend their time and talents to our restoration process. The bulk of the work was done by Grave Stone Matters.

All too often gravestones from the early to mid-1800s have fallen down, are broken, and/or buried under the sod. Once uncovered they can be pieced together and serve as proper memorials to those long dead.

Dozens of mid-nineteenth century gravestones in Section 2 were repaired in the summer of 2016. The once deteriorated hillside is gleaming with memorials to mostly Irish immigrants who proudly carved their county and parish of origin in stone, making them a valuable resource to genealogists.

There are eighty-two Civil War veterans buried in this section. All of the veterans' stones have been either replaced or restored.

This restoration work was funded privately through individual and corporate donations. Memorial upkeep and cleaning remain the responsibility of the lot owner. However, when it becomes clear there are no longer family members to care for the monuments, the cemetery can allocate donated funds toward repair and preservation. Hundreds of monuments marking the graves of those long dead and forgotten have been properly cared for by contractors hired by the cemetery, or in some cases, by the historian working with a team of volunteers.

▼ *The Sisters of the Good Shepherd left the Albany area many years ago and the gravesite for sisters of the late nineteenth and early twentieth centuries were long forgotten until the summer of 2016. The large marble statue and two rows of small marble stones were in complete disarray and blackened by pollutants to the point that they were illegible. A phone call to the Sisters' home in Astoria, New York, telling them of the situation resulted in a generous donation to the cemetery specifically to restore the lot as a corporal work of mercy. The work was completed with excellent results.*

▶ *Dressed in plastic for about a week to allow mortar to cure at a slower rate, the line of small stones on the Sisters of the Good Shepherd lot will once again stand upright, sturdy, and clean. The stones and Christ the Good Shepherd monument in the background were cleansed of pollutants with D/2 Biological Solution. This cleaning agent has become an industry standard and part of a best practice approach to gravestone restoration.*

Once broken messes, the thirteen small stones in front of the Christ the Good Shepherd statue are upright and stable.

◀ A lamb that has been exposed to the elements for 150 years shows no sign of its original, intricate detail. This lamb marks the grave of a toddler who died of unknown causes.

▶ A late winter storm shrouds the ground in Section 2, making the graves seem even quieter and more peaceful. Many of the gravestones in this section have seen over 180 winters, and yet their inscriptions are still legible.

◀ Dozens of marble stones were unearthed in Section 2 and pieced back together. Most mark the graves of Irish immigrants. Lambs often mark the graves of children, although not always, as in this case. John: 1:29—"Behold the Lamb of God, which taketh away the sin of the world."

Honoring the Dead, Celebrating Our Nation, and Reaffirming Our Faith:
Flag Day Ceremony, June 14, 2016

In 2010, it was discovered that twenty-seven soldiers and sailors buried in two VA-owned lots did not have grave markers. All of the men—one Spanish American War veteran, twenty-three World War I veterans, and three World War II veterans—died between 1955 and 1963 in the Stratton VA Hospital in Albany. It is uncertain why their graves were left unmarked, but it is likely that none of them had next of kin to follow through on an application for a veteran's memorial marker. The St. Agnes historian began searching for military service records and easily found service records for thirteen of the men. However, fourteen veterans remained in unmarked graves, their service records missing in the National Archives.

The process of obtaining grave markers for the remaining soldiers and sailors was made difficult for two reasons: military service records and proof of honorable discharge were not easily located, and the VA in Washington, DC put restrictions on the application process by requiring the next of kin to make the request. No next of kin could be located. The VA has since lifted that restriction and once again we were able to submit applications for veterans with no known next of kin—but we still need proof of service. The cemetery enlisted the assistance of staff at the Stratton VA Hospital and together we gathered enough information to apply for grave markers

◀ *Laying of the Commemorative Wreath by Very Reverend Donald L. Rutherford, Major General, U.S. Army, Retired.*

▶ *Historian Kelly Grimaldi receiving the flag. Her father, a twenty-year veteran of the United States Navy, looks on.*

▶ *World War II Naval veteran Joseph Nicpon reading the American's Creed.*

for eleven out of the remaining fourteen unmarked graves. The last three of the fourteen veterans had no proof of service even though we know two of them served in World War I and one in World War II. Two private citizens purchased markers for the remaining three veterans and our mission to mark the graves of twenty-seven soldiers and sailors was finally complete after six years.

A full military honors ceremony to honor these men and rededicate the VA lots was held on Flag Day, June 14, 2016. Flag Day was an appropriate time to honor these men. It marks the adoption of the Stars and Stripes as our national flag by the Continental Army in 1777, and it is the day that marks the founding of the United States Army. President Woodrow Wilson officially established June 14 as Flag Day in a proclamation issued 100 years ago on June 14, 1916.

▲ *Cemetery manager Luke McGarry removing the large Latin Cross that was once on top of the receiving vault. Decades of weather caused the foundation to shift, throwing the stone off center.*

▶ *This cross once adorned the top of the receiving vault that deteriorated over the years. Receiving vaults were used in cemeteries to store bodies in the winter before grave digging became mechanized. In the late 1980s, cemetery grounds crew found the cross and base in a ravine located along the cemetery's southern border. They recognized its historical significance and spent hours using heavy equipment to retrieve it and reassemble it by the entrance of the cemetery where it stands today.*

THESE SACRED GROUNDS

Joe Ferrannini, proprietor of Grave Stone Matters, practicing his craft. Joe has restored thousands of gravestones all over the country. In 2014, he restored the Golden lot, one of the earliest established lots in St. Agnes Cemetery. The large Gothic-style monument for the Golden Family was erected circa 1870.

The Owen Golden lot was completely restored in 2014, with the exception of the Latin cross belonging on top of the Gothic spire.

▲ This is an original gravestone for a Civil War veteran who died in 1879. St. Agnes Cemetery is the final resting place for more than 525 veterans of the Civil War. In 2007, a massive restoration effort commenced to restore or replace the marble monoliths marking the graves of men who fought for the Union cause. To date, more than 400 stones have been restored and at least 100 replaced.

▶ With her hands over her heart, flowing locks of stone that seem to be blowing in the wind and her heavenward gaze, this beautiful marble sculpture of a young female is one of the prettiest in the cemetery. The Pickett lot, purchased in 1884, is a fine example of Victorian tastes in funerary art. Smaller marble stones in the background were all restored in the summer of 2015.

THESE SACRED GROUNDS

The African Burial Ground

On June 5, 2005, construction work on Route 32 near the Menands Village and Town of Colonie line uncovered a burial ground estimated to have been established in the 1700s to early 1800s. Archeologists discovered thirteen sets of remains (one set of remains was found in 1998 during a separate construction project) and sent them to the New York State Museum for bioarchaeological analysis.

Concluded in 2010, the analysis found the remains to consist of six women, one man, two children, and five infants who were determined to be mostly of African ancestry, with one person of mixed Native American and African ancestry. The burial ground was part of a large estate, known today as Schuyler Flatts, that was owned by the Colonial era Schuyler family. All evidence supports the fact that these fourteen people were once enslaved by this branch of the Schuyler family.

The Schuyler Flatts Burial Ground Project Committee worked with archaeologists, artists, woodworkers, and historians, combining their resources with many partners to create burial containers and a multidenominational ceremony to honor these individuals. In 2015, St. Agnes Cemetery donated this burial

▲ *The multidenominational burial ceremony.*

◀ *All faiths and all ethnicities came together to pay their respects to the fourteen people who were denied their freedom while they lived in the late 1700s. Enslaved in life, they are slaves no more.*

site and the Town of Colonie funded the tombstone and marker in honor of these fourteen people who deserved to be buried with dignity and respect in sacred ground for all time. On June 18, 2016, a memorial ceremony of the highest honor was held and the remains, enclosed in custom-designed burial vaults, were laid to rest. The symbol on the burial vaults and African Burial Ground gravestone is called Sankofa. It is an African word from the Akan tribe in Ghana.

▲ *Albany Mayor Kathy Sheehan, surrounded by children, places a flower on the African Burial Ground's gravestone.*

▲ *Young people from neighboring communities served as pall bearers. As each burial container was handed to them by Kristin McVeigh of McVeigh Funeral Home, Albany, NY, the young men solemnly walked up the carriage path to the final resting place now called the African Burial Ground.*

▶ *The solemn interment ceremony.*

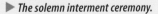

▶ The symbol on the African Burial Ground gravestone is called Sankofa. It is an African word from the Akan tribe in Ghana. The literal translation of the word and the symbol is "it is not taboo to fetch what is at risk of being left behind." This is the back of the stone for the people removed from the Schuyler Flatts Estate and reburied on Founders' Hill.

▲ Gravestone installation by Albany Diocesan Cemeteries Operations Staff (left to right): James Cavallaro, Bob Barrows, Tim Lane, and Luke McGarry.

THESE SACRED GROUNDS

THE WHOLENESS OF THE LIVING IS
DIMINISHED WHEN THE ANCESTORS
ARE NOT HONORED.

Conclusion

WRITING THIS BOOK, uncovering some of the stories long buried in St. Agnes Cemetery, and choosing photographs offering the best pictorial narrative of what this rural Catholic cemetery is all about has been both a challenge and pure joy. I feel privileged to put into words some of the things that have made and continue to make this Victorian-era cemetery a very special place to so many people over the past fifteen decades. You, the reader, picked up this book and read the stories of people who lived long ago. You looked at the pictures and read the captions and undoubtedly could understand, appreciate, or sympathize in one way or another the universality of the human condition. We are all connected: those who have died, you, and me. Cemeteries provide us with a tangible space where we are able to reflect on the beauty of life while standing among the essence of the deceased.

I once found an inscription on an eighteenth century gravestone that read: "Death is a debt to nature due, that I have paid and so must you." Not a very comforting thought, is it? What differentiates St. Agnes Cemetery from earlier established cemeteries is its mission to comfort people grieving for loved ones—not resign them to the knowledge of a finite existence on Earth. It is a faith-based mission. Believers in Christianity know that death is not a debt to nature, but a means to move forward into the realm of the Lord for everlasting life in His dwelling.

Detail from the steps of the McArdle Family monument.

▲ An old Copper
Beech stump serves as
a Victorian-era plant-
er on Founders' Hill.
The restored Quinn lot
and Preston lot down
the hill gleam brightly
in the sun.

▶ Ornately forged
bronze doors lock
in stoic guardian-
ship, protecting the
remains of Albany's
wealthiest citizens.
They could not take
their money with
them so they left
reminders of their
social status in the
form of elaborate
and expensive private
mausoleums that we
can all enjoy visiting.

Then I saw a new heaven and a new earth; for the first

heaven and the first earth had passed away, and the sea was no more.

And I heard a loud voice from the throne saying,

"See, the home of God is among mortals.

He will dwell with them;

they will be his peoples,

and God himself will be with them;

he will wipe every tear from their eyes.

Death will be no more;

mourning and crying and pain will be no more,

for the first things have passed away."

And the one who was seated on the throne said,

"See, I am making all things new."

— Rev. 21:1a, 3-5a

Beneath the sod in St. Agnes Cemetery lay the remains of thousands of
people. I hold dear to my heart these sacred grounds. It is comforting for me to
know that when it is my time to leave my earthly dwelling, my body will rest here
on Founders' Hill in peace with so many others who have passed before me.

Kelly Grimaldi

Historian, Albany Diocesan Cemeteries

About the Author

KELLY A. GRIMALDI holds a master's degree in history from the University of Albany with a concentration in the study of funerary art, architecture, and burial trends in Europe and America. Her interest in old cemeteries brought her to historic St. Agnes Cemetery as a volunteer in 2008. In 2010, she was offered the position of historian for Albany Diocesan Cemeteries and eagerly accepted the challenge of the position. She had no predecessor to give her guidance on what it is exactly that a cemetery historian does. It was new territory. Over the years, Kelly developed programs in the arts and humanities that draw people of all ages into the cemetery for painting lessons, art exhibits, history tours and lectures, and a number of special events and ceremonies all open to the public. One of her goals early on was to start compiling stories about some of the people buried in St. Agnes Cemetery in anticipation of writing a book for the 150th anniversary of the cemetery's founding. This is her first book.

 CapitalDistrictCemeteries.org